19.95

TIME
The **100** Most Influential People Who Never Lived

Lucille Ball, as Lucy Ricardo, in a typical jam on *I Love Lucy*, 1951

MANAGING EDITOR Richard Stengel
ART DIRECTOR D.W. Pine
DIRECTOR OF PHOTOGRAPHY Kira Pollack

The **100** Most Influential People Who Never Lived

EDITOR/WRITER Kelly Knauer
WRITER Ellen Shapiro
DESIGNER Ellen Fanning
PICTURE EDITOR Mark Rykoff
RESEARCHER Tresa McBee
COPY EDITOR Bruce Christopher Carr

TIME HOME ENTERTAINMENT
PUBLISHER Jim Childs
VICE PRESIDENT, BRAND AND DIGITAL STRATEGY Steven Sandonato
EXECUTIVE DIRECTOR, MARKETING SERVICES Carol Pittard
EXECUTIVE DIRECTOR, RETAIL AND SPECIAL SALES Tom Mifsud
EXECUTIVE PUBLISHING DIRECTOR Joy Butts
DIRECTOR, BOOKAZINE DEVELOPMENT AND MARKETING Laura Adam
FINANCE DIRECTOR Glenn Buonocore
ASSOCIATE PUBLISHING DIRECTOR Megan Pearlman
ASSOCIATE GENERAL COUNSEL Helen Wan
ASSISTANT DIRECTOR, SPECIAL SALES Ilene Schreider
DESIGN AND PREPRESS MANAGER Anne-Michelle Gallero
BRAND MANAGER Michela Wilde
ASSOCIATE PRODUCTION MANAGER Kimberly Marshall
ASSOCIATE BRAND MANAGER Isata Yansaneh
ASSOCIATE PREPRESS MANAGER Alex Voznesenskiy

EDITORIAL DIRECTOR Stephen Koepp

SPECIAL THANKS
Katherine Barnet, Brad Beatson, Jeremy Biloon, Stephanie Braga, Susan Chodakiewicz, Rose Cirrincione,
Brian Fellows, Jacqueline Fitzgerald, Christine Font, Jenna Goldberg, Hillary Hirsch, David Kahn, Amy
Mangus, Nina Mistry, Dave Rozzelle, Ricardo Santiago, Adriana Tierno, Vanessa Wu, TIME Imaging

*The following entries in this volume were written by Ellen Shapiro: Norman Bates, Lisbeth Salander,
Candide, Barbie, Betty Crocker, the Marlboro Man, Rosie the Riveter, Mary Poppins, Peter Pan,
Katniss Everdeen, Nancy Drew. All other unsigned entries were written by Kelly Knauer.*

ISBN 10: 1-61893-071-0
ISBN 13: 978-1-61893-071-2
Library of Congress Control Number: 2013938445

We welcome your comments and suggestions about TIME Books.
Please write to us at: TIME Books, Attention: Book Editors, P.O. Box 11016, Des Moines, IA 50336-1016

To order any of our hardcover Collector's Edition books, please call us at 1-800-327-6388.
Hours: Monday through Friday, 7 a.m.–8 p.m., or Saturday, 7 a.m.–6 p.m., Central Time

Lift-off *Actors dressed as P.L. Travers' immortal nanny Mary Poppins took to the air during the opening of the Olympic Games in London in 2012*

Contents

Introduction

The Characters Among Us

Hamlet and Don Quixote, Darth Vader and Batman, James Bond and King Midas: these people seem part of our everyday lives, but that's an illusion. They do not exist and never have existed, yet their lessons and lore are a pervasive part of our approach to life.

Fictional characters are all around us, the secret sharers of our hopes and fears, the companions of our childhood, the signposts that mark the waystations in our lives: from Santa Claus and Cinderella to Nancy Drew and Holden Caulfield; from Mary Richards, Lucy Ricardo and Cliff Huxtable to (gulp) King Lear. Along with Shelley's poets, these characters are the unacknowledged legislators of the world.

Each of us has met a Cassandra, a naysayer who can find a dark lining in the whitest of clouds. We've known Scrooges who delight in their own misanthropy, Don Juans for whom every woman is a prey to be stalked, Peter Pans who refuse to grow up, long after their boyish ways have lost their charm. And we're still arguing over whether each of us is hard-wired with our very own Oedipus complex, or whether Sigmund Freud was overreaching when he looked back to Greek tragedy to issue his universal analysis.

Fiction offers a wonderful way for the creators among us to distill the essence of basic human traits into pure form, then bring them to memorable life in the guise of an outsized exemplar. Along that trail, as characteristics become characters, a certain magic enters the equation, and the result is a person who never existed, yet whom we feel we have always known: the young lovers Romeo and Juliet, the adorable ditz Lucy Ricardo, the lusty old goat Falstaff.

Of course, these avatars of human traits have a wonderful advantage over real humans: they are willfully, delightfully one-sided rather than multifaceted. Dorothy Gale is ever plucky, Robinson Crusoe ever resourceful, Darth Vader ever villainous—no boring Tuesday mornings for him. And in the midst of the story, we live

in their moments. "These people and situations are nearly as immediate and urgent as our 'real' lives," says Jessica Winter, who contributed pieces on King Lear and Mrs. Rochester. "We root for or against them, use them as inspirational models or cautionary tales, take the words out of their mouths and use them as jokes or mantras. How blurry the line becomes between their worlds and ours is a measure of the artistry and craftsmanship that went into creating the characters."

The residue of that artistry is influence. And at TIME, parsing influence is part of our editorial tradition, so we decided to explore the avatars who embody our faults and virtues, the heroes and villains who serve as our inspirations and warning signs. Our model was TIME's annual list of the 100 Most Influential People in the World—and the result is this volume, *The TIME 100 Most Influential People Who Never Lived.*

As we assembled our newest take on the TIME 100 list, we followed some of the lessons learned in the past. The influence we sought to identify could be exercised for good or for ill, and our list would include monsters like Hannibal Lecter as well as inspiring role models like Jo March. As always, we aimed to include a diverse, wide-ranging cast of characters that would cut across lines of gender, race, ethnicity and culture—but there is no doubt our list reflects the familiarity with European and American culture shared by our intended readers.

We established some basic rules early on. The list would be confined to humans, which meant eliminating such beloved characters as Mickey Mouse, Snoopy, Yoda and Frodo Baggins. That decision also excluded gods and divinities—so farewell to Zeus, Thor, Apollo and Dionysus, as well as to such personified superhuman forces as Father Time and Mother Nature.

And since our list was designed to stimulate thought rather than anger, we ruled out all religious figures. Noah, Moses, Job—their stories are memorable, but it's not the province of this book to rule on whether their

Moira Shearer danced the title role in Frederick Ashton's ballet *Cinderella* in 1948

lives were real or the product of ancient imaginations. However, the list does include three figures from the New Testament who are frequently cited in modern life and who are entirely fictitious, originating in parables told by Christ: the Prodigal Son and his father, and the Good Samaritan

As we assembled the list, we invited readers of *Time.com* to share their views, and we received a hefty response. Turns out Santa Claus is a popular gent— *d'oh*. Sherlock Holmes and James Bond were close behind him in popularity, but some surprises emerged. Turns out the Dude from *The Big Lebowski* doesn't merely abide—for *Time.com* readers, he rules. But who cast so many votes against including Robin Hood? Hedge-fund traders? Fans of Ayn Rand's champion of the virtues of selfishness, John Galt? It wasn't surprising that readers felt little sympathy for Franz Kafka's

victim of a shadowy bureuacracy, Josef K., an entry suggested by TIME book critic Lev Grossman. But it's the role of book critics to champion excellence where they find it, so perhaps Grossman's choice may inspire a few readers to pick up *The Trial* and meet Kafka's character.

And that's our hope for this book: that it will encourage close encounters with fascinating new characters, shake up dinner-table conversations and generally raise a ruckus. Why include Anna Karenina rather than Emma Bovary? Why Robinson Crusoe and not Lemuel Gulliver? Why Batman and not Spider-Man? Our list reflects our preferences, and it's been a pleasure to put it together. Go ahead and quibble with it: we invite you to take the test of compiling your own list of the 100 most influential people who never lived. As Candide and Pollyanna would assure you, that's one test on which all the answers will be correct. —*By Kelly Knauer*

Heroes & Villains

King Arthur

Origin: British folklore; Geoffrey of Monmouth's
History of the Kings of Britain, **circa A.D. 1136**

Like several other characters in this book, King Arthur may not be entirely fictitious: it is highly possible that this great exemplar of a just monarch was based on a real king of the Dark Ages, a British warlord who fought for the rights of his people against Saxon invaders. But even if there was at one time such a leader, he is a victim of identity theft, his exploits overshadowed by the thick layers of myth and lore that have encrusted his fictional doppelgänger.

And what myths they are, many of them first put forth by the chronicler Geoffrey of Monmouth in his 12th century history of British Kings. His tale of Arthur Pendragon and his rise to power is rich with unforgettable images and figures. There is the memorable test presented by Excalibur, the sword in the stone, and the wise aid of the wizard Merlin, model for Tolkien's Gandalf, and there is the wooing of the fair Guinevere.

Later tales by the 12th century French poet Chrétien de Troyes and the British chronicler Wace introduce the Round Table, a rare symbol of democratic equality in a caste-choked society. The wonderful Knights of the Round Table are the forerunners of every band of good guys that followed: Robin Hood and his Merry Men,

the Dirty Dozen and the Avengers. Chrétien wrote of the tragic but necessary downfall of Camelot, the ideal state sundered by man's inescapable frailties: pride, jealousy and lust.

Somewhere along the way, as Arthur's very British story was transformed to express the new European worldview of chivalry, the figure of Arthur was hijacked: he was reduced to playing the cuckold, an impotent prop in the tale of the forbidden passion of the gallant French knight Lancelot and Guinevere. But Arthur rose again in the Romantic era of the 19th century, when Sir Walter Scott, Alfred Lord Tennyson and others created a mania for all things medieval.

British novelist T.H. White's witty, rich novel of Arthur's story, *The Once and Future King* (1958), scoured the rust off the old tale. Lerner and Loewe's musical adaptation of White's yarn, *Camelot* (1960), and its association with the Kennedy Administration, ensured Arthur's don't-let-it-be-forgot appeal. And when the Monty Python crew unveiled the 1975 film *Monty Python and the Holy Grail* and followed it in 2005 with the musical comedy *Spamalot*—well, as they say in Hollywood: Arthur has legs for miles.

King Arthur
Scarlett O'Hara
Hannibal Lecter
Norman Bates
Indiana Jones
Lara Croft
Rodion R. Raskolnikov
Michael Corleone
James Bond
Dr. Faust
Dr. Frankenstein
Candide
Lisbeth Salander
Travis Bickle
Kunta Kinte
Robin Hood
Captain Ahab
Don Quixote
Don Juan
John Galt
Big Brother
Odysseus
Achilles

Arthur in a circa
1900 illustration,
artist unknown

Scarlett O'Hara

Origin: Margaret Mitchell's novel *Gone With the Wind*, 1936

I got my copy of *Gone With the Wind* (hardback) on my 13th birthday. I tore off the wrapping, dropped to the floor and read it straight through. My older sister had received her copy years before, but when I had begged for it she only shook her head, saying I was much too young. I had watched the movie on network television every year, doled out over two nights. I had a life-size poster of Clark Gable as Rhett Butler on my bedroom door. I had the Madame Alexander doll of Scarlett O'Hara and fussed over her hair and wardrobe as if I were Mammy. I was in love with Scarlett before I read the book, and I was considerably more in love with her after.

I never gave a thought to Scarlett's being manipulative or conniving, though certainly she was. She was the gravitational center of the universe. Tara was her home, her land, and she was going to keep Tara together regardless of whether or not the world was falling apart. As far as my 13-year-old self was concerned, Scarlett was a role model, not that she was teaching me to marry for

necessity while casting an eye toward other women's husbands but that through her example I learned the importance of assessing the situation and getting the job done. Scarlett taught me that when the chips were down and many lives required saving, including your own, the best person to rely on was yourself. She was focused and unapologetic. I admired that.

I wonder if there are still any girls today looking to Scarlett for guidance, or if they've found everything they need in Beyoncé, another young woman who seems equipped to both bat an eye and walk through a wall. Certainly *Gone With the Wind* was ancient history when I got my hands on it in 1976, but it is considerably further removed from the world today. Still, when I hear the phrase "As God is my witness," I think of Scarlett gnawing on dirty radishes in a field. No reader, no moviegoer, no doll owner, ever thought that Katie Scarlett O'Hara was going to starve. She was too resourceful for that. All these years later, it's the resourcefulness I remember.   —*By Ann Patchett*

Vivien Leigh as Scarlett, *Gone With the Wind*, 1939

Hopkins as Lecter, 1991

Hannibal Lecter

Origin: Thomas Harris' 1981 novel *Red Dragon*

The thing about monsters is that they're supposed to be monstrous. They're supposed to jump out from doorways, claw their victims' flesh with the dank cold breath of the Underworld. Pure Evil. Blackness. Physicality. Then there's Hannibal Lecter, Thomas Harris' infamous, twisted serial killer, the subject of cult fascination and unending awkward giggles. When we first see him in *The Silence of the Lambs,* there's a clarity of purpose about him, a beauty, standing perfectly still in the bright cold light of his prison cell. All in white, blue eyes shining, waiting for that special someone to step into his web. "Hello, Clarice."

With his metallic voice and all penetrating stare, Lecter slithers into a vulnerable young woman's head and whispers the truths of her psyche. Cunning in his cruel thirst for intimacy whatever the form, he just wants to inflict pain, to penetrate beyond the bars, to connect. One-way dominance. And she lets him, hungry for that father she lost, for those precious keys he's dangling, for the impossible power of his gaze. Sound like boyfriend material? Not quite. How about a vicious cannibal psychopath who boasts his treatment of a presumptuous census taker, "I ate his liver with some fava beans and a nice Chi-ant-i."

We know the breadth of his killer résumé but can't help cheering him on. Why? Why do we love Lecter so? Because he's real. He's honest. Because, when shown respect, he is capable of giving so much. Because he never whines about the provenance of his dark spirit, no "my father beat me," or "my mother never loved me." He just *is,* in all his delicious duality. Utterly monstrous. Utterly human. And all that evil … I don't know … Just feels like love to me.

—*By Jodie Foster*

Lara Croft

Origin: Eidos Interactive's 1996 video game, *Tomb Raider*

Far back in the misty dawn of the video-game era—the 1980s, in other words—a pair of zany Italian plumbers created by Japanese design genius Shigeru Miyamoto became the first video-game heroes whose stage was a TV screen. Nintendo's Mario and Luigi became beloved icons of video gaming, yet, like the early games they appeared in, they were barely two-dimensional. But as both the technology of such games and the aspirations of their creators continued to evolve, the characters on the screens began to take on the depth and texture of real life.

Enter Lara Croft, who in 1996 became a rare female intruding on a world dominated by such male fantasy figures as Duke Nukem, and in which the vast majority of those directing the action on the other end of the controller were young males. Croft's British creators solved that problem by making Croft an ogle-worthy babe whose bustline defied both gravity and logic. Then they went a step further, giving Croft a fun backstory as the daughter of a British lord and helping themselves to a generous slice of the Indiana Jones franchise, presenting her as a brainy archaeologist with a flair for tomb-raiding.

By 1999, when she was only three years old, Lara's first three games had sold 17 million copies, and she sported all the attributes of modern celebrity: a Lara Croft comic book, a Lara Croft candy bar, a Lara Croft action doll. Older aficionados could dig into *Generation X* author Douglas Coupland's tome *Lara's Book* for a hipper take on all things Croft.

By 2001, fans could ante up to watch Croft on the big screen, as a well-cast Angelina Jolie laced up Lara's big boots and became the world's sexiest archaeologist. A 2003 sequel followed, but times have been hard for Lara in recent years, as the films stopped and her game sales slumped. Not to worry: her new 2013 game is a hit, and Hollywood's own archaeologists, ever alert to the possibilities of a reboot, will resurrect her any day now.

Peter Lorre as Raskolnikov in a 1935 version of *Crime and Punishment*

Rodion R. Raskolnikov

Origin: Fyodor Dostoyevsky's 1866 novel, *Crime and Punishment*

From Dante's *Inferno,* where hell seems a good deal more interesting than heaven, to Milton's *Paradise Lost,* where Satan gets all the best lines, to Shakespeare's *Othello,* where Iago's intrigues are more compelling than Othello's virtues, writers have learned fiction's dark secret: the allure of evil trumps the banality of good. Yet in Fyodor Dostoyevsky's *Crime and Punishment,* the author passes rapidly over his main character's evil deeds—the pointless murders of an innocent old woman and her half-sister—to explore their psychological consequences.

Dostoyevsky understood punishment not as a concept but as bitterly lived experience. A parlor radical in his youth, he was arrested, along with dozens of utopian associates who questioned the regime of Czar Nicholas I, and put through a mind-bending form of psychological torture: he was convicted of treason, sentenced to death, blindfolded and put in front of a firing squad—only to be given a reprieve at the last moment and sentenced to four years of exile in a Siberian prison camp.

The author's years in chains deepened and darkened his view of the human condition and inspired his creation of Raskolnikov, the impoverished former student whose love of idealistic concepts outpaces his love for the messy realities of human life and leads him to justify his murders as an expression of his self-declared superiority over the common man. In Raskolnikov, Dostoyevsky traced the chilling trajectory of the sort of evil that begins with grandiose visions of the superhuman, only to end in the death camps of Hitler's Germany, the gulag of Stalin's Russia and the horrors of the Great Cultural Revolution of Mao's China. The guilty young man is the dark prophet of the 20th century's false gods.

Al Pacino as Michael Corleone in *The Godfather,* 1972

Michael Corleone

Origin: Mario Puzo's 1969 novel, *The Godfather*

In the uneasy relationship between Hollywood films and the novels they are based on, the film often plays the role of the parasite, sucking the nuance, depth and voice out of the book as it blows it up to big-screen, mass-audience proportions. But in some rare cases, when a film is touched by genius, it can transcend its source material—as was the case when director Alfred Hitchcock turned Robert Bloch's *Psycho* into a modern classic, or when actor Anthony Hopkins made Hannibal Lecter one of history's most compelling villains. In just this way, author Mario Puzo, director Francis Ford Coppola and actor Al Pacino teamed up to create, in young Mafia don Michael Corleone, a modern character who can take his place as one of fiction's greatest tragic figures.

After decades in which American gangsters were portrayed as little more than goons with guns, Puzo's 1969 novel and Coppola's 1972 film of *The Godfather* set organized crime within the rich pageant of the Italian migration to America, revealing a world in which the values of family, honor and tradition are corrupted by crime—yet whose characters are so compelling that they seduce the audience into sympathy for their warped views. In the sequel film, *The Godfather: Part II* (1974), Coppola and Puzo focus on Corleone's rise to power as the don of a vast criminal Mob—and on tracing the chilling accommodations such power demands. In the film's climactic scene, Corleone, who has devoted his life to protecting both his personal family and his Mob family, is forced to choose between the two after his brother Fredo betrays him. His impossible choice—to kill his own brother in the name of the larger family—makes Michael a tragic hero/villain of towering proportions, bound to the destiny forged by the corrupted values of honor and tradition he has embraced.

Brand Bond *At right, a bevy of movie Bonds, minus one-shot George Lazenby in* On Her Majesty's Secret Service, *1969. Below, Sean Connery and Daniela Bianchi in* From Russia with Love, *1963*

Roger Moore Timothy Dalton Pierce Brosnan Daniel Craig

James Bond

Origin: Ian Fleming's 1953 novel, *Casino Royale*

The most remarkable feat of James Bond, Agent 007, is that he has survived. It's not so surprising that he has lived through falls from great heights into icy waters after being shot from a speeding train *(Skyfall)* or a laser beam that is seconds away from dividing him in half from the groin up *(Goldfinger)* or being dropped into a pool of hungry sharks *(Live and Let Die)*. He is, after all, British.

But this is a character who should have faded into irrelevancy decades ago. Let's take stock: he has a horrible carbon footprint. He drinks openly during working hours. As an employee of the taxpayer, his abuse of government property—including cars, planes, Rolexes with miniature saws, exploding pens and individual jet packs—frankly verges on fraud. And that's before we get to his woman problem.

How is a government official with a string of what we would now call sex crimes on his résumé, who has literally made women take bullets for him, still a viable cultural force? At the very least should he not have been drummed out of the business by a sexual harassment suit? (Moneypenny, hello?)

And yet, here he is, 60 years on, an extra-cheesy icon in a lactose-intolerant business. There have been 23 Bond films, more than any other hero has been afforded. And age has not enfeebled his appeal: the last seven Bond films each made more money than the one before it. He's so hardy that he's survived six changes of actor, one of whom wasn't even an actor but a male model. Caring about country and duty is so five superheroes ago, but Bond has kept at it, through all weathers. Perhaps his venerability is what saves him. In a world in which heroes come and go, it's comforting to know there's one with an irrevocable license to thrill.
—*By Belinda Luscombe*

Sean Connery

13

Marguerite, Faust and Mephistopheles, from Charles Gounod's opera *Faust,* circa 1900, artist unknown

Dr. Faust

Origin: Ancient German folktales, first printed version published in 1587 in the chapbook *Historia von D. Johann Fausten*

Is this the fate that launched a thousand hits? The sticky end of John (or Johann) Faustus, Fausten or simply Faust, has inspired playwrights, poets, painters, moviemakers, classical musicians and rockers and created a global brand for the trade-off of integrity for personal aggrandizement. The Faustian pact described in the first known version of the tale, a slim volume printed in Germany in 1587, sees an ambitious scholar literally sell his soul for knowledge and power. In Christopher Marlowe's haunting play, premiered in the late 16th century, that transaction, signed in blood as demanded by Lucifer's emissary, Mephistopheles, condemns Faustus, after 24 years of lording it on earth, to submit helplessly to eternal damnation. The Faust conceived by German poet Johann Wolfgang von Goethe in the 19th century also dies, but the penitent spirit of Marguerite, a woman he has despoiled, intervenes to lead his soul to heaven.

What makes these narratives so potent isn't their outcomes. Whether or not Faust is redeemed, his example serves as a warning of the limits of temporal power and material wealth. This is a story that helps to explain the air of boredom that clings to the super-rich as they consume their way around the world, the

dissatisfaction of the sexual predator after a conquest, the frustration of the dictator who kills at will but can't quench opposition. There are modern-day Fausts sitting in deep-carpeted offices atop global financial institutions and multinational companies. They look like the embodiments of success, yet each new day confronts them not only with the inevitability of mortality but also with the limitations of the life all their money and influence have bought them.

The legend redefines hell, not as a prison of fire and brimstone that awaits sinners after death but as a reality that envelops the living if they forget that happiness cannot be purchased at the expense of others. Goethe's *Mephistopheles* describes hell as "the eternal empty distance," while Marlowe's Lucifer, asked why he is apparently able to leave hell at will, replies, "Why this is Hell, nor am I out of it." He continues, "Think'st thou that I, who saw the face of God / And tasted the eternal joy of Heaven / Am not tormented with ten thousand Hells/ In being depriv'd of everlasting bliss?" Hell—a state of being that threatens all of us—tastes like disappointment and feels like loss. And there's more than a glimpse of heaven in the beauty of Marlowe's words, the cadences of Goethe's verse.

—*By Catherine Mayer*

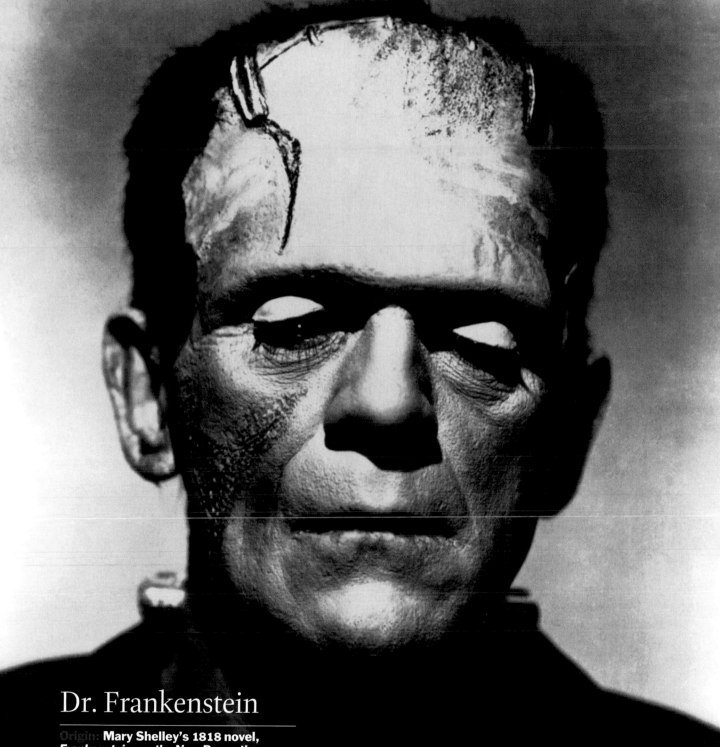

Dr. Frankenstein

Origin: **Mary Shelley's 1818 novel,**
Frankenstein; or, the New Prometheus

No, the figure shown above isn't Dr. Victor Frankenstein; it's the creature assembled by that eminent scientist from the body parts of deceased humans, then electrically galvanized into life. The creature haunts our dreams, yet there is great pathos surrounding him, for he is a deeply unnatural being, and he finally turns on his creator, killing Dr. Frankenstein's fiancé and pursuing the scientist to the Arctic Circle in hopes of taking revenge upon him.

If the "wretched devil" created by the scientist is unforgettable, it is the figure of his creator who is at the center of Mary Shelley's novel, which was written as part of a contest dreamed up by the 18-year-old British woman, her married lover and future husband, the poet Percy Shelley, and others. The author claimed that the vision of Dr. Frankenstein and his monster came to her in a waking dream. The resulting novel is a deeply prophetic work that anticipates a world in which humanity's increasing mastery of the powers of science unleashes not wonders but horrors. In the figure of Dr. Frankenstein, we see the old tale of the Faustian bargain updated—with science cast as the devil.

Engraving by Charles Monnet
from a 1778 edition of *Candide*

Candide

Origin: Voltaire's 1759 novella, *Candide, or Optimism*

Ho-hum, another dusty volume of the Western canon, another masterpiece we were told to appreciate in high school. Except *Candide* is refreshingly, hilariously modern. A nonstop poke-in-the-eye to royalty, religion and pompous intellectuals, it has enough sex and violence to make Quentin Tarantino smile. Voltaire's slim satire puts its characters through an astonishing array of calamities, including but not limited to earthquakes, disembowelments, rapes and shipwrecks.

At the center of the action is Candide, the kind and exceptionally innocent illegitimate nephew of a German baron. Candide's gullible mind is molded by his blowhard tutor, Dr. Pangloss, who is modeled on the German mathematician and philosopher Gottfried Wilhelm von Leibniz. Pangloss espouses the "philosophy of optimism," the belief that God has created the "best of all possible worlds" and that everything—including the most horrifying acts of man and nature—happens for the greater good. Leibniz had indeed made such claims early in the 18th century.

Voltaire, as a father of the Enlightenment, will have none of that; for one thing, he had been deeply touched by the horrors unleashed on the Portuguese people by the Lisbon earthquake of 1755. The merciless satirist shamelessly skewers Pangloss's cockeyed optimism by marching his innocents through the mud. After Candide is banished for canoodling with the baron's daughter, he roams the earth like some 18th century Forrest Gump, trying to hold onto his good heart from one absurd horror to the next. His rationalizations are endearingly droll. "I have seen the worst," he says. "But a wise man, who since has had the misfortune to be hanged, taught me that all is marvelously well; these are but the shadows on a beautiful picture."

What saves everyone in the end is a different philosophy altogether, at once ancient and refreshingly up to date: Go back to the land, and you shall be free. Candide and the friends he has found end up on a small farm in Turkey, where they cultivate their garden, eat pistachios and finally understand that hard, simple work will banish the mumbo-jumbo in their heads.

Lisbeth Salander

Origin: Stieg Larsson's 2005 novel, *The Girl with the Dragon Tattoo*

How could a ferocious, emotionally damaged cybergenius who looks as if she's "just emerged from a weeklong orgy with a gang of hard rockers" become a worldwide cultural sensation? Lisbeth Salander, a.k.a. *The Girl with the Dragon Tattoo, The Girl Who Played with Fire* and *The Girl Who Kicked the Hornets' Nest,* is the unlikely yet captivating heroine of Stieg Larsson's *Millennium* franchise, which since 2005 has spawned sales of more than 60 million books in 50 countries, four feature films in two languages (so far), an H&M clothing line and countless online musings.

An amalgam of contradictions, Lisbeth is barely 5 ft. tall but battle ready with multiple face-piercings, elaborate body ink and "hair as short as a fuse." Her enemy is "men who hate women" (the original title of Larsson's first book) and, more personally, the deeply corrupt legal guardian who repeatedly raped her, then had her declared insane and locked in a mental ward. That she survived is remarkable; that her revenge was almost as horrific as his violation is one of the more intriguing, and possibly psychotic, hallmarks of her complicated persona.

For all her fighting skills, Lisbeth's real superpowers begin with a keyboard. A researcher and hacker of uncanny skill, she knows there's no firewall too impervious for her to penetrate, no incriminating information that is beyond her reach. She first gets to know *Millennium* magazine editor Mikael Blomkvist—her comrade-in arms in the hunt for sexual predators—by breaking into his computer, one of her only avenues for benign human connection.

Whatever labels she attracts, Lisbeth is never cartoonish. No matter how punk she goes, we're fascinated by her vulnerability and her pursuit of a glimmer of trust in her very dark world. Her furious defiance of the violence done to her—and to many other women—gives her a reality that other action heroes can't match. When Lisbeth Salander suffers, it's for horrific crimes as real as the morning news.

Noomi Rapace as Salander, 2009

Robert De Niro played Bickle in 1976

Travis Bickle

Origin: Martin Scorsese's 1976 film, *Taxi Driver*

Reviewing Martin Scorsese's dark masterpiece *Taxi Driver* in TIME on its premiere in 1976, film critic Richard Schickel declared, "There is a certain kind of urban character who, however lightly we brush against him, instantly leaks the psychopathy of everyday anguish all over us. He is a man working in a menial job that brings him into constant, envious touch with people more fortunate than he, a man enraged by the bad deal life has given him but unable to articulate that rage. Instead, he is given to fantasies ranging from the glumly sexual to the murderously violent. He is, finally, a man of muttered imprecations and sudden, brooding silences; which of these moods is most alarming is hard to say."

The character of Travis Bickle, brilliantly portrayed by Robert De Niro in the film written by Paul Schrader, captured all the grit and menace of New York City street life in the 1970s. But in the decades since, Bickle has come to represent a broader type than Schickel's urban weirdo. He now seems a forerunner of a figure Americans are all too familiar with today: the lonely, unstable young male who turns to violence to make a social statement, to achieve notoriety, to seek some kind of revenge against a world he believes has wronged him. In Bickle, it's possible to see the seeds of the 25-year-old assassin of John Lennon, of another 25-year-old who dressed up as an executioner and shot up a Colorado theater, of the 20-year-old who prowled the corridors of a Connecticut grade school and took the lives of 26 people. Travis Bickle once seemed a snapshot of a disturbed person at a specific time. But in retrospect, he seems to have offered a compelling preview of horrors that are now all around us.

Kunta Kinte

Origin: Alex Haley's 1976 novel, *Roots*

Almost a century and a quarter after Harriet Beecher Stowe forced Americans to confront the issue of slavery in her epochal 1852 novel, *Uncle Tom's Cabin,* author Alex Haley created a work whose impact was frequently compared with Stowe's famed work. His 1976 novel *Roots* became a national sensation when it was adapted into an eight-part 1977 mini-series on ABC and commanded one of the largest audiences in TV history. As the co-author of *The Autobiography of Malcolm X,* Haley had helped tell one of the seminal black stories in modern American life. In *Roots,* he dug deep into the past, exploring the history of Africans in America—and paving the way for a day in which the term African American is worn as a badge of honor.

Haley's genealogical search took him back to West Africa. In Gambia he encountered an aged griot—a tribal oral historian—who traced Haley's lineage back centuries to when his distant ancestor, Kunta Kinte, was snatched by slavers in 1767. In Haley's generation-spanning novel, Kinte is brought to the U.S. via the dread Middle Passage, is renamed Toby and suffers all the horrors slavery has to offer. Yet the character, indelibly portrayed by LeVar Burton, passes on the name "Kunta Kinte" to his children, and the legacy of the name becomes a refrain throughout the book, binding black Americans together and linking them to their African heritage.

In Kunta Kinte, Haley gave American blacks an authentic hero to embrace. Along the way—huddled in a semicircle in their living rooms around that electronic-age griot, the TV set—Americans of both races discovered that they shared a common heritage, however brutal, and that the ties that linked them to their ancestors also bound them to each other.

Burton played Kunta Kinte
in the 1977 TV mini-series *Roots*

Robin Hood, 16th-century woodcut

Robin Hood

Origin: English folktales, first collected in *The Gest of Robyn Hode,* circa mid-15th century

Robin Hood is a folk hero whose appeal is summed up in his unforgettable mission statement: "to rob from the rich and give to the poor." It's fitting that he was not created by a single author; rather, he embodies the collective dreams of the common people who created him.

The story of Robin Hood embraces many other populist fantasies. He and his Merry Men, a colorful band of outlaws, represent the bonds of brotherhood and equality that we all aspire to—and it's important that Maid Marian and other women share an equal place in the band. Sherwood Forest near Nottingham is the perfect home for this group of free spirits uncorrupted by society's laws: it is a Garden of Eden, British-style, a verdant sanctuary where the town's flawed values cannot intrude. In later versions of the story, Robin is a disgraced nobleman in hiding, but that version is a gussied-up retelling of stories that were originally inspired by hatred and resentment of the nobles and religious orders who oppressed the poor.

Robin Hood is an early manifestation of a figure that Americans have often embraced: the outlaw who is morally superior to the corrupt values of the prevailing culture he resists. "To live outside the law you must be honest," Bob Dylan declared, and in Robin Hood we find the forefather of heroes from Butch Cassidy and the Sundance Kid to John Galt, Winston Smith and Han Solo: the savior disguised as a criminal who strings up his bow and fires a Cupid's arrow of hope into our hearts.

Captain Ahab

Origin: Herman Melville's 1851 novel, *Moby-Dick; or, the Whale*

One way to identify a truly universal character is the Pictionary test. Sure enough: if you outline a crude peg leg on a stick figure, it won't be long before someone names Herman Melville's immortal antihero—the obsessive, godlike man who will chase the white whale that devoured his limb to the ends of the earth. They call him Ahab.

The journey of this grand, unraveling ship captain who seeks improbable vengeance has kept *Moby-Dick* on lists of best novels for almost a century. There's more to Melville's epic than Ahab—it's an ode to adventure at sea; a handbook on New England whaling; a survey of religion, class, race and money. But Ahab is the keystone. He embodies humankind's bloody desire for whatever is believed to be justice. His story is made of life's largest questions: death and life and judgment. And though scholars compare "Old Thunder" to other narrative giants, from King Lear to Job, Ahab remains as singular as he is myopic, the Lord of the Leviathans, who shares a name with an ancient Israelite king doomed to die by the Lord's decree.

When *Moby-Dick* was published in 1851, reviewers called it tiresome and labeled its language "mad." It sold only 500 copies in the United Kingdom, where it was first released. But after Melville's death in 1891, the literati took a second look and by the mid-20th century, *Moby-Dick* was recognized as an American masterpiece. First editions are priced today at upwards of $80,000.

The long, digressive work still isn't an easy book. BBC produced an online audio version called the Big Read. Almost 125,000 people listened to the first chapter; just over 12,000 of them made it to the last installment. But that still represents a sea of readers who understand that it's worth the effort to know the cultural anchor that is Ahab. Because he has become the archetype for all sea commanders and a first reference for maritime parodies. Because he has inspired films, songs, bands, fine art and fan fiction. Because his name is shorthand for maniacal obsession and unyielding pursuit. "Mark ye, be forewarned," Captain Peleg tells Melville's narrator, Ishmael, as he prepares to sail with the ivory-legged legend. "Ahab's above the common."

—By Katy Steinmetz

Ahab, illustration by Rockwell Kent, 1930

Illustration by G. Franz, 1883

Don Quixote

Origin: Miguel de Cervantes' novel *The Ingenious Gentleman Don Quixote de La Mancha,* **published in two parts in 1605 and 1615**

For one of fiction's most noted losers, Don Quixote has enjoyed a long winning streak in Western culture. Apparently not content with being the protagonist of Europe's first great novel, the Knight of the Woeful Countenance has escaped the traces of his creator, Miguel de Cervantes, and become an all-purpose symbol of the high-minded believer in ideals who is fated to wage losing battles, over and over again, with the pesky windmills of reality.

A large part of the aging nobleman's appeal is his other half, Sancho Panza, the down-to-earth manservant who provides the ballast to Quixote's ethereal visionary and who is one of literature's greatest sidekicks. As George Orwell wrote in 1941, "If you look into your own mind, which are you, Don Quixote or Sancho Panza? Almost certainly you are both. There is one part of you that wishes to be a hero or a saint, but another part of you is a fat little man who sees very clearly the advantages of staying alive with a whole skin."

Toying with questions of reality and illusion, and portraying his hero as both a pathetic figure of folly and an admirable exponent of man's highest ideals, Cervantes strikes a very modern stance in his masterpiece. The dreamer of La Mancha may not have beaten his windmills, but he slew an entire epoch: through him, Cervantes drove a spike through the Middle Ages' exaggerated concerns with chivalry and illusionary worlds. Goodbye to those angels dancing on pinheads. Goodbye to Dante's nine levels of hell. Welcome, modernity. Firmly announcing the advent of the Renaissance, Cervantes portrays humans as the measure of all things, using Sancho Panza's blunt maxims to take the starch out of those who think too much, dream too much, talk too much. "A closed mouth catches no flies," he declares.

Douglas Fairbanks as Don Juan in a 1934 film

Don Juan

Origin: Tirso de Molina's play *The Trickster of Seville and the Stone Guest,* **first published circa 1630**

Don Juan is the lusty libertine, the conquistador of the boudoir, the serial thriller, the Hall of Fame pitcher of woo. In our modern, vaguely industrial term, he is a womanizer, and many have fallen under his spell. Byron, Baudelaire and Pushkin portrayed him in verse; Mozart immortalized him in the 1787 opera *Don Giovanni,* still a staple on the world's stages. He has been painted by Delacroix and Dalí. And oddly enough, this man who embodies carnality and lust seems to hold special appeal for those known for toiling with their minds: among those who have contemplated Don Juan's navel—and parts in the vicinity—are George Bernard Shaw, Soren Kierkegaard and Albert Camus.

Like so many of the figures in this book, Don Juan is an incomplete man, stripped of most human drives to accentuate the one he embodies: the libido. In *Man and Superman,* Shaw placed Don Juan in hell, and the seducer's tale of conquests is unfinished if it doesn't include his comeuppance and punishment. In the work that introduced him to the stage, the Spanish monk Tirso de Molina's play *The Trickster of Seville and the Stone Guest,* the cad shares top billing with the agent of his doom. The stone guest is the statue of Don Gonzalo, the father of Doña Ana, one of Don Juan's conquests. Gonzalo had been slain by Don Juan after he protested the debauchment of his daughter: now the statue has returned to life to achieve the father's revenge. Like the stone guest, Don Juan also keeps coming back for more: portrayed by Johnny Depp in the 1995 film *Don Juan DeMarco,* he will be played by Joseph Gordon-Levitt in the 2013 film *Don Jon.*

September 2, 1946

(1)

I "The Calendar"

"Who is John Galt?"

The light was etting, and ~~into~~ ~~the~~ ~~better~~ ~~of~~ Eddie Willers could not distinguish the bum's face. The bum had said it simply, ~~without~~ without expression. But from ~~the~~ far at the end of the sunset ~~and~~ street, yellow ~~caught~~ glints ~~caught~~ ~~his~~ his eyes, and the eyes looked straight at Eddie Willers, ~~and~~ mocking and still; as ~~a~~ if the ~~thought~~ ~~that~~ ~~the~~ ~~and~~ question had been addressed to ~~that~~ the causeless uneasiness within him.

First page of Rand's manuscript of *Atlas Shrugged*

24

John Galt

Origin: Ayn Rand's 1957 novel, *Atlas Shrugged*

Who is John Galt? This innocent question is the engine that drives the plot of Ayn Rand's magnum opus, *Atlas Shrugged*. At first the question seems little more than a teasing refrain intended to draw us into the novel, but as the story proceeds, the author builds terrific suspense around these four simple words. And when we meet Galt at last, he is so compelling that we feel rewarded rather than cheated by Rand's narrative bait. Galt, you see, is … but why spoil it?

Atlas Shrugged is a fantastic novel—that is to say, it is a work of high fantasy, whose characters are about as plausible as Spider-Man and Wonder Woman. The heroes of Rand's work are gifted, heroic individualists doing battle with the villains who would smother personal honor, genius and aspiration beneath a thick collectivist goo of mediocrity. Rand was 52 when the book was published, but her characters seem to have sprung full-blown from the forehead of a 14-year-old boy. A Nordic pirate? Cool! A South American copper magnate? Weird! A genius industrialist who creates a new form of metal, and whose supersmart, supersexy, superrich mistress designs a nifty bridge to display the powers of the blue-green superstuff? Dude!

Yet it's no matter that Rand's characters are little more than puppets in her mitts, for *Atlas Shrugged* is not intended to be a real novel. Instead, it is a mighty polemical blast against the forces that Rand—a refugee from Stalin's Russia—most feared. In Rand's world, there are no nuances, no complex human motives. Instead, there are heroic "makers" and villainous "takers." Her equivalent is not Leo Tolstoy; it is Thomas Paine. Her work, which in recent years has found many new adherents, is, for many, a highly persuasive political manifesto. This unillustrated volume may be history's most influential comic book.

Big Brother, from a 1965 BBC telecast of *1984*

Big Brother

Origin: George Orwell's 1949 novel, *1984*

Winston Smith is the narrator and hero of George Orwell's dystopian novel about the dangers of totalitarianism. But the highly fallible Smith is designed by his creator to stand for unremarkable middle-managers everywhere, and Smith yields the spotlight in the novel to its unforgettable villain, Big Brother, the artificial totem created by the totalitarian government of a future Britain (Airstrip One) as a personification of the power of the state over the individual. Big Brother is not real, but then again, the Joseph Stalin who directed a vast chain of forced-labor camps in the U.S.S.R. was also using a pseudonym: the "man of steel" in the Kremlin was born Joseph Jughashvili.

Big Brother's agents of terror are the Thought Police, abetted by a vast system of monitoring gear, including two-way TV screens that allow the state to spy on private activity. Orwell was a onetime socialist who became a fervent anti-Stalinist and devoted his life to defying totalitarianism. His warnings ring truer than ever in today's world, where video surveillance cameras allow authorities to monitor us in ways that Big Brother might envy, and digital applications like Photoshop help us alter history and reality with a few clicks of a mouse. (The flip side of such fears, of course, is the ability of surveillance cameras to serve the cause of justice, as when those in Boston helped identify the 2013 marathon bombing suspects.) There is no happy ending in *1984*: its would-be hero, Smith, finds his spirit broken under torture, and he bows to the reality the state enforces: "He loved Big Brother."

Odysseus lashes himself to the mast. Roman mosaic, 3rd century A.D.

Odysseus

Origin: Homer's *Odyssey*, 8th century B.C.

The figures of Odysseus and Achilles speak to the long span of Western cultural memory. Both characters are thought to have existed as Greek myths before they appeared in the two works attributed to the legendary poet Homer, the *Odyssey* and the *Iliad,* which scholars date to the 8th century B.C. In the days of Homer, Greek listeners are believed to have enjoyed these stories in episodic form as songs played to the accompaniment of a stringed instrument. Today, we're more likely to encounter them on the big screen at a local multiplex. Either way, the resourceful wanderer Odysseus and the mighty warrior Achilles have been putting fannies in the seats for 2,800 years now.

Many scholars declare that the *Iliad* is Homer's masterpiece. But for modern audiences, the *Iliad* can seem skimpy on plot—this saga of the siege of Troy doesn't even include the Trojan horse—while the picaresque adventures of the ingenious Odysseus are among the most memorable in fiction. On his long journey to return to his wife Penelope, Odysseus (Ulysses, to the Romans) blinds the one-eyed cyclops Polyphemus, lashes himself to the mast of his ship to escape the irresistible song of the Sirens and tangles with the sorceress Circe, who turns his shipmates into swine. Canny, capable and cool, Odysseus is the template for every wandering hero—including Leopold Bloom in James Joyce's *Ulysses* and the Civil War soldier W.P. Inman in Charles Frazier's 1997 novel, *Cold Mountain.* As the Romans said, quoting the Greek physician Hippocrates: *Vita brevis, Ars longa.*

Achilles

Origin: Homer's *Iliad*, 8th century B.C.

Achilles is one of Western culture's greatest warrior figures—which makes it all the more ironic that he is also one of Western culture's biggest crybabies. The mainspring that drives the plot of Homer's *Iliad* is the wrath of Achilles, directed at the Greek commander and his superior officer, Agamemnon, as forcefully announced in the opening lines of the poem, when Homer invokes the muse to help him tell his tale. As translated by Stanley Lombardo, the work begins:

> *Rage: Sing, Goddess, Achilles' rage*
> *Black and murderous, that cost the Greeks*
> *Incalculable pain …*

Indeed, to the despair of students everywhere, Achilles spends long sections of the poem sulking in his tent, as tens of thousands of Greek soldiers lay siege to the city of Troy, where the King's son Paris has stashed that paragon of beauty, Helen.

Achilles is gifted with great power by virtue of his divided nature: he is the son of the mortal King Peleus and the goddess Thetis and is thus a demigod. Surprisingly, the *Iliad* does not mention the memorable attribute that makes him a sympathetic and tragic figure: in a later telling of his tale, by the Roman poet Statius in the 1st century A.D., we learn that Thetis dipped the infant Achilles in a sacred pool that made his body invincible to injury, except for a tiny section at the rear of his foot where his mother held him during this enchanted baptism—the Achilles heel.

That term remains with us as an emblem of humanity's inescapable flaws, just as Achilles, for all his posturing as the Sultan of Sulk, remains with us as an exemplar of courage and bravery, whether portrayed by Brad Pitt in the 2004 film *Troy* or sketched by writer Madeline Miller in her 2012 best seller *The Song of Achilles.*

Pitt as Achilles in *Troy*

Archetypes

Uncle Sam

Origin: Disputed. Many historians believe the character was based on an early 19th century military supplier, Samuel Wilson

He is the uncle you can't hide in the basement: the one everyone knows, everyone loves—and everyone worries a little bit about. He is Uncle Sam, the symbol for a nation, its people, their vast, far-reaching government and all that is good and bad and that comes in between.

But most of all, Sam represents an indigenous American spirit, a doughty national character who has endured for more than 200 years now. What makes Sam different is that he started out real and then became a fiction. The first Uncle Sam was probably a federal contractor from Troy, N.Y., by the name of Samuel Wilson, who made a killing providing dried beef and other victuals to the U.S. Army during the War of 1812. Wilson branded his beef barrels with the letters *U.S.,* in deference to his client, but the young military recruits who cracked them open for lunches and dinners came to refer to those containers as "gifts from Uncle Sam." Newspapermen quickly adopted the nickname, in part because they were badly in need of another way to refer to the United States, then locked in war for the second time in 40 years with England,

which had its own convenient namesake, John Bull.

Political cartoonist Thomas Nast picked up the theme in the late 19th century, turning Sam into a lanky, top-hatted figure with striped pants and a white goatee; by the time the Army was looking for ways to boost recruiting during World War I, Sam had become a potent (and more grim-faced) father figure who could point a finger and say, "I want YOU for U.S. Army." By then, Sam was always seen decked out in some form of red, white and blue. Stars were usually part of the uniform.

If Britain's Bull is a stuffy, slightly overweight English gentleman, America's Sam is tireless, abstemious, perhaps a bit naive—and also given to occasional excess. Uncle Sam is still used interchangeably with his more pejorative handle, Uncle Sugar, a reminder that when Washington finally gets around to doing something, it usually overdoes it. That Sam is descended from a military provisioner has surely helped him survive all that history. Two hundred years on, he seems as young as ever.

—*By Michael Duffy*

Uncle Sam
Sherlock Holmes
The Good Samaritan
Falstaff
Shylock
Barbie
Betty Crocker
Santa Claus
Ebenezer Scrooge
Hiawatha
The Marlboro Man
Rosie the Riveter
Jay Gatsby
Mrs. Rochester
King Midas

U.S. Army recruiting poster, 1917,
illustration by James Montgomery Flagg

Sherlock Holmes

Origin: **Arthur Conan Doyle's 1887 novel *A Study in Scarlet*, published in a magazine**

I n 1886 a 27-year-old London doctor with budding literary ambitions sat down to write a detective story. For inspiration he had Charles Dickens' Inspector Bucket and Edgar Allan Poe's C. Auguste Dupin, as well as a real-life model, his former colleague Joseph Bell, a Scottish physician who was a pioneer of forensic observation. He tried out a few different names for his sleuth—Sheridan Hope, Sherringford Holmes—before he settled on Sherlock Holmes. (The detective's able assistant, Dr. John Watson, was originally called Ormond Sacker.) Arthur Conan Doyle finished writing *A Study in Scarlet* in a matter of a few weeks.

Holmes may have had predecessors, but he was very much an original. His personal habits are untidy. He sleeps late. He is prone to depression and mania and indulges in tobacco and even cocaine. He is utterly ignorant of anything that doesn't directly relate to his work—in *A Study in Scarlet* he claims to have been unaware that the earth revolves around the sun.

But Holmes' mind is a thing of absolute crystalline order. His powers of observation and deduction are enormous, and his memory for apparently trivial facts peerless—he has written an entire monograph on the variations between different kinds of tobacco ash. He's almost as imposing physically as he is mentally. He's skinny, with a nose that Doyle describes as "hawk-like," but he's over 6 ft. and a superb boxer. In *The Adventure of the Speckled Band* (1892) he shows that he can bend a metal poker with his bare hands.

Holmes is single-mindedly devoted to the craft of detection, and his personal relationships are few. His closest friend is his partner Watson (although Holmes never actually utters the phrase "elementary, my dear Watson"). He has a landlady, the loyal Mrs. Hudson, and an older brother, Mycroft, whose intellectual powers are even greater than his own. Holmes maintains a squad of street urchins, the Baker Street Irregulars, who gather information for him. He has only contempt for romantic attachments, but he does permit himself a profound admiration for Irene Adler, a beautiful former opera singer who boasts the rare distinction of having outwitted him.

Holmes was very much a product of his age: we think of the Victorians as stiff and proper, but they had an intense and morbid fascination with crime, particularly with murder, and to them Holmes was practically a secular saint. The idea that a man of genius, through the relentless application of logic and science, could bring light and clarity to the darkest and most terrifying human secrets was an infinitely appealing one.

And it still is. Holmes remains one of the best-known and most beloved figures in popular literature, and he holds the Guinness World Record for having been portrayed more times on film and TV than any other character. Sadly, the only person who seems to have disliked Holmes was Doyle himself, who longed to be known for his more serious literary efforts. He even went so far as to kill off his creation in 1893 in *The Final Problem*—but the public outcry was so loud that eight years later he relented and brought Sherlock Holmes back to life. —*By Lev Grossman*

Supersleuth *Below, the silhouette of Basil Rathbone as Holmes in a 1939 film. At bottom, a 1910 poster promotes a new Holmes story in the* Strand Magazine.

At left, a 1901 illustration for a Holmes tale in the Graphic *magazine*

THE BEST SHERLOCK HOLMES ADVENTURE

IN THE SEPTEMBER STRAND MAGAZINE

The Good Samaritan, artist unknown

The Good Samaritan

Origin: The New Testament's Gospel of Luke, 10: 29-37

In the shattering days after bombings at the 2013 Boston Marathon killed three innocent people and wounded hundreds more, many Americans joined Massachusetts Governor Deval Patrick in saluting "the firefighters and police officers and EMTs who ran toward the blasts, not knowing whether the attack was over—and the volunteers and other civilians who ran to help right alongside them." There is a name for such people—Good Samaritans—and the name comes from a parable in which Christ tells of a young Jewish man who was beaten, robbed and left for dead on the road. After a priest and an aristocratic Jew ignored the man's pleas for help, it was a Samaritan, a member of a religious group shunned as a minority in Israel, who bound up his wounds and paid for his care at an inn.

Christ's parable is so memorable that its hero has become a byword for anyone who comes to the aid of another. That's fine, but it's not really what Christ had in mind. His parable challenges us not only to help others but also to practice the most demanding act of the Christian faith: to love and help even our enemies. As we learned from the tragic events in Boston, Good Samaritans are all around us, caring people coming to the aid of strangers. But in an age in which so many voices urge us to demonize others, what we really need is not just Good Samaritans. We need Better Samaritans.

Falstaff

Origin: William Shakespeare's play *Henry IV, Part 1,* **circa 1596-97**

Patriot Sam Adams and presidential brother Billy Carter are proof: when they put your name on a beer bottle, you've hit the big time. A further step up the ladder of renown is the moment when your name becomes an adjective. And only a few characters have reached the pinnacle of inspiring an opera by Giuseppe Verdi. Sir John Falstaff, Shakespeare's immortal blowhard easily achieved that rare trifecta. He is the scenery-chewing star of Verdi's 1893 comic opera *Falstaff,* which perhaps inspired the Lemp Brewing Co. of St. Louis to name its once popular brew after him ten years later. And a look through *Webster's Third New International* dictionary finds him perfectly pegged as a person who is "fat, jovial, humorous, dissolute."

For a man who boasts of his laziness, Shakespeare's burly, bawdy braggart keeps himself busy staking claim to as many of the seven deadly sins as possible. Lust, gluttony, envy, greed, sloth, pride: you can check them off in order. But though Falstaff has been known to pitch a fit, he isn't guilty of the seventh sin, wrath—and that's the secret of his charm. Like his 20th century counterpart, Jackie Gleason's Ralph Cramden, the elderly knight is in on his own joke, for beneath all the bluster and bombast, he is the owner of a sweet, sweet heart. That's why he's lovable—so lovable, in fact, that Queen Elizabeth I, supposedly amused by his antics as the sidekick of the future King Henry V in two of Shakespeare's history plays, is said to have asked the bard to make him the star of his own show. Shakespeare complied, creating *The Merry Wives of Windsor* to feature Falstaff in love.

Shakespeare, known for snitching his plots, practiced identity theft in this case. Falstaff was based on and initially named for a noted rebel against both church and state who was executed in 1417, Sir John Oldcastle. When Lord Cobham, his descendant, heard of the Bard's plans, he intervened and won a name change for one of history's most buoyant characters.

Stephen Richardson in Verdi's *Falstaff* at the Sydney Opera House in 2006

Shylock

Origin: William Shakespeare's play *The Merchant of Venice*, circa 1596-98

To explore Shylock, we invited two great modern interpreters of the role to share their views on his character.

A hooked nose, a kippah, foreign robes, a set of scales, a raised knife over the exposed breast of a noble gentleman. Shylock!

When I first played Shylock for the Royal Shakespeare Company in 1979, a theater critic began his review of the production by asserting that there were two ways of playing Shylock: as a downtrodden member of a despised race, evil and bloody in his pursuit of revenge against the Christians who loathe him, or as a proud, contemptuous Jew, morally and ethically superior to his Christian tormentors. This critic did not like my performance because it failed to fit either of these stereotypical categories.

For actors who love performing Shakespeare, this assessment is ludicrous. The compulsion these performers feel is in large part because of the diversity, complexity and life found in Shakespeare's characters, the qualities that make them worth exploring over and over again. I have played Shylock five times. The first time, aged 12, I read it out loud in the classroom of my inspirational English teacher, Cecil Dormand, at Mirfield Secondary Modern School. The most recent time was a 2011 RSC production of *The Merchant of Venice* set in Las Vegas. With each new experience, a human being emerged from the text: gregarious, charming, deeply religious, witty, garrulous, brilliant and funny. And yes: angry, deeply resentful, lonely, controlling, manipulative, reckless, opportunistic and finally accepting and humble ... a survivor.

Instead of identifying him simply as a great tragic hero/villain, let's put him in a very human context. Shylock is a single parent raising his only child, Jessica, without any female influence or support. He loves her desperately but trumping his love is the fear that he may lose her, and so he restrains and restricts her and in doing so, of course, makes it inevitable that he will lose her. Jessica's deceased mother, Leah, is mentioned only once, when Tubal, Shylock's friend, tells him that the eloping Jessica gave a ring she had stolen from her father for a monkey. Shylock's response is, for me, one of the two overwhelming moments of infinite sadness in the play: "Out upon her. Thou torturest me, Tubal. It was my /turquoise. I had it of Leah when I was a bachelor./ I would not have given it for a wilderness of monkeys."

In that speech one word leaps off the page and into one's heart: *bachelor*. There was a time when Shylock was a young man in love and he gave his beloved, Leah, a ring. Shakespeare's genius is in opening up Shylock's history for us in this way and for a little moment illustrating that he was not always angry, controlling and resentful but was once youthful, loving and romantic.

And the other moment? It is toward the end of the Act IV trial scene. Given a choice between death and abandoning his religion, Shylock chooses the latter with the words "I am content." All my life I have loved Shakespeare's simplest speeches more than the great purple passages. "I pray you, undo this button," says the dying Lear. "I hope all will be well," says Ophelia, as everything is about to get so much worse. And perhaps the most potent: "Oh, she's warm!" says Leontes, taking the hand of a marble statue of his dead wife.

Shylock is a great and multifaceted character, though he only appears in five scenes. He is not Lear, or Hamlet, or Macbeth, but the mind that made these towering characters made Shylock too. —*By Patrick Stewart*

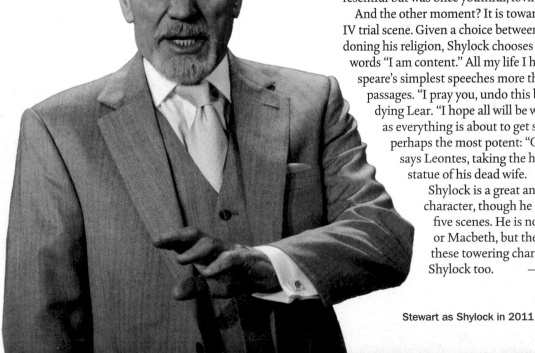

Stewart as Shylock in 2011

In film noir movies, if you were a crook between jobs and in need of cash, you went to a shylock to borrow it. When in the world did crooks have the time to read Shakespeare? I always figured they were busy with their molls, drinking, smoking, talking dirty and wearing hats. But why shouldn't they have a reading hour when everyone stopped what they were doing to discuss the classics?

In *Guys and Dolls,* Sky Masterson reveals his encyclopedic knowledge of the Bible—every hotel room has a Gideon, he says, and since he lives in hotels, that's what he reads. But that's not the whole truth.

If the Good Book wasn't very good, he wouldn't waste his time. In fact, it's a great piece of literature; according to Harold Bloom, the Bible and the works of Shakespeare are the two towering accomplishments in world literature.

The mystery is how Shylock became flesh and blood. Mary Shelley's Frankenstein's monster is as real as the golem, but neither has been assimilated as other than a creature, a bogeyman. Shylock, on the other hand, absolutely exists; he is part of our society. The mention of his name brings him instantly to mind as a living human being. Shakespeare's accomplishment with Shylock goes far beyond his Jewishness. Shylock is every one of us who has suffered at the hands of injustice, and his magnificent "Hath not a Jew eyes" speech in Act III is equalled by his less well known courtroom speech in Act IV. Listen to his response when the judge asks him to forgo the debt that is owed him:

> *You have among you many a purchased slave*
> *Which like your asses and your dogs and mules,*
> *You use in abject and in slavish parts,*
> *Because you bought them. Shall I say to you,*
> *"Let them be free, marry them to your heirs?*
> *Why sweat they under burdens? Let their beds*
> *Be made as soft as yours, and let their palates*
> *Be season'd with such viands?" You will answer*
> *"The slaves are ours." So do I answer you:*
> *The pound of flesh, which I demand of him*
> *Is dearly bought; tis mine and I will have it.*
> *If you deny me, fie upon your law!*
> *There is no force in the decrees of Venice.*
> *I stand for judgment! Answer: Shall I have it?*

As in Shylock's Act III speech, Shakespeare has written a very simple, clear and modern argument for dignity, for equality. He has endowed Shylock with an envious courage and intellect, as well as a healthy sense of humor. He is a man we are curious about, might like to spend some time with. But above all, he is real—a living being, perhaps more alive than many of us.

This sort of creative impulse seems so distant from today's "art scene": there is little evidence of the skill and craft required to create any lasting artistic contributions in the piles of crushed baby carriages, the rows of suitcases, the garage sales and sleeping bodies that inhabit the most famous galleries in the world.

Even worse, there seems no end in sight as critics give erudite descriptions of junk. As the divine Lily Tomlin once said, while holding a can of Campbell's soup in one hand and a picture of a can of Andy Warhol's painting of a Campbell's soup can in the other, "This is *soup,* and this is *art.*"

Fifteen minutes of fame ain't worth the candle. Shylock has passed into the language because he speaks to us, and through us. I long for art that focuses on a universal expression of humanity: we don't need more junk, there is quite enough around already, some of which I've been part of, but I never pretended it was art. I count on Shakespeare, among others, to help me restore my soul when I come back from the trenches. As Shylock says, "I stand for judgment! Answer: Shall I have it?"

—*By F. Murray Abraham*

Barbie

Origin: Created by Ruth Handler in 1959

Born Barbie Millicent Roberts, March 9, 1959, at the New York Toy Fair, wearing a zebra-striped bathing suit, open-toed heels and her signature topknot ponytail. Accessories included gold hoop earrings and blue-tinted shades.

Birth mother Ruth Handler, who scandalized the doll market—then dominated by cherubic babies—by introducing a supremely buxom teenager into the mix. She based her creation on Bild Lilli, a popular German sex toy, and named it after her daughter Barbara.

Legal guardian Mattel Inc. of El Segundo, Calif., founded in 1945 by Handler, her husband Elliot and Harold Matson.

Body stats Height: 11.5 in. Weight: 7¼ oz. Measurements translated to human size: about 39-18-33 in.

Race/ethnicity Caucasian, African American, Asian, Native American, Indian, African and Hispanic—seven skin tones in molded plastic. More than 40 different nationalities, including Jamaican, Peruvian and Thai.

Career One hundred thirty jobs, including teen fashion model, rock star, doctor, race-car driver, veterinarian, paleontologist, aerobics instructor and Marine Corps sergeant. In the '60s she went to the moon—four years before Neil Armstrong.

Wheels Private jet, Rockers Race Car, Vespa, Austin-Healey 3000 MKII, Pop Up Camper, Dream 'Vette, Pink Beach Jeep, to name but a few.

Love life After dating Ken for 43 years, Barbie dumped him on Feb. 12, 2004. Mattel's press release stated, "One thing is for certain—Barbie® and Ken® will always remain the best of friends." Seven Valentine's Days later, a press release declared, "Barbie® is Back in the Arms of Ken®!"

Fan base More than a billion Barbies have been bought in 150 countries, more than 7.6 million have liked her on Facebook, and more than 150,000 follow her on Twitter.

Controversies Feminists (and moms) charge that she encourages body hatred in girls and promotes eating disorders. The Iranian government banned her for her "destructive cultural and social consequences."

Income A gazillionaire, Barbie and her brand haul in $3 billion worldwide each year.

Legacy The Rorschach test of the toy world, Barbie has generated more delight, anger and ink than most human icons. Is she the "plastic princess of capitalism"? The ultimate career woman? A simple bimbo? Or should we all calm down and heed the immortal words of Barbie's handlers, the Mattel p.r. department: "She's a doll, people ..."

Solo in the Spotlight
Barbie, 1960

1930s

1950s

1960s

1970s

1980s

1990s

A bevy of Bettys
Times change, and so do Betty's hairstyles and skin tones, but she magically remains about 32 years old

Betty Crocker

Origin: Introduced in 1921 by Gold Medal Flour

There was a time in our great land when getting a cake to rise was an iffy proposition. Cookbooks were rare, pan sizes irregular and oven temperatures temperamental. In 1921, Washburn Crosby (soon to be renamed General Mills), the purveyors of Gold Medal Flour, ran a promotion and were astonished at the number of homemakers seeking cooking advice.

Enter company adman Samuel Gale, who, with a gleam in his eye, created Betty Crocker. (The name *Betty* was chosen for its All-American cheeriness; *Crocker* saluted a retiring executive.) Betty started out as a "Dear Abby" for the kitchen-challenged, soothingly dispensing recipes and practical advice. Each and every letter was "personally" signed by Betty—in reality company secretary Florence Lindeberg.

Before long Betty had a wildly successful radio show that helped families cook cheap, balanced meals during the Depression and World War II. FORTUNE magazine said the show "did for [Betty's] career in commerce what it did for Franklin D. Roosevelt's in politics," and in 1945 she was deemed the second best-known U.S. woman after a living, breathing Eleanor Roosevelt.

By now Betty was everywhere. Her iconic cake mixes were introduced in 1947, and in 1950, the heyday of the American housewife, the *Betty Crocker's Picture Cookbook* was published. "Big Red" outsold the Bible in its first year and is now in its 11th printing. A TV show and cooking schools followed, as well as a popular test-kitchen tour in Minneapolis, where some visitors were crushed to learn that Betty didn't exist.

It's not surprising that a lot of people thought Betty was real. She's had a face since her first portrait in 1936—and she always seems to keep up with the current styles. In 1965 she had pearls and a flip, vaguely reminiscent of First Lady Jackie Kennedy. In 1986 she got her ears pierced. And to celebrate her 75th anniversary in 1996, Betty became less white bread: a digital composite of 75 women gave her olive skin and brown eyes to reflect America's growing diversity.

For an imaginary woman, Betty has taken her share of knocks for pushing overprocessed food and for her image as an overly dutiful hausfrau. But unlike some of today's domestic goddesses, Betty is an antidiva who has always kept herself in the popular mix. And by doing so, she retains her shelf life as one of the greatest advertising icons in history.

Santa Claus

Origin: Folktales based on the life of St. Nicholas, a 4th century A.D. bishop

Have you been naughty, or have you been nice? The jolly old soul who keeps a list of such data sprang from a real religious figure. St. Nicholas was a generous bishop of Myra, now Demre, in today's Turkey; among other good deeds, the patron of pawnbrokers is said to have restored life to three children who had been chopped up by a butcher and marinated in brine.

But the history is fuzzy, and the man we know today as Santa Claus is really a secular miracle-worker conjured into existence by poets, painters and advertisements. In 1823 Clement Clarke Moore, a lyrical professor of literature and divinity, told us that his eyes twinkled and his dimples were merry, that when he laughed, his belly shook like a bowlful of jelly. Illustrators like Norman Rockwell and companies like Coca-Cola helped refine our image of the red-suited, black-belted legend, whose reindeer fly him all over the world in a single night so he can deliver presents—and eat chocolate-chip cookies.

The modern Santa Claus is a one-man stimulus package. Every year he inspires new plots, jingles and tchotchkes. Every year, his image helps Salvation Army bell-ringers win donations from rivers of shoppers, who are on their way to patronize stores that rake in some 40% of their earnings during the holidays. For this, the retailers surely thank him as much as cultural Scrooges curse him for being a driver of commercialism and excess, particularly among the world's 2 billion gift-giving Christians.

For non-Christians, Santa may be a symbol of exclusion, a painful early lesson about In groups. But his greatest influence is in the happiness felt by millions of children who peel back the days of their Advent calendars, distracted and wild for his arrival. For them, Santa is an introduction to benevolence, to getting what you deserve—and to being under constant surveillance. (He sees you when you're sleeping. He knows when you're awake.) The age that these believers find out that Santa isn't real becomes a way to compare upbringings. And the illusion of a kindly old man with a bag of toys becomes a rite of passage, one they will pass on to their own children, be they naughty or nice.

—By Katy Steinmetz

38

Groeten van
St. Nicolaas!

Christmas Greetings

Gruss vom Nicolo!

MERRY CHRISTMAS

Representations of Santa Claus over time

Illustration from a 19th century edition of *A Christmas Carol,* by E.A. Abbey

Ebenezer Scrooge

Origin: Charles Dickens' 1843 novella, *A Christmas Carol*

Along with Clement Clarke Moore, poet of "The Night Before Christmas," Charles Dickens did more to give us our jolly holiday than any writer since St. Luke. The great Victorian novelist wrote tens of thousands of words in celebration of roaring fires, roasted geese and happy faces beaming in "the season of immortal hope" on "the birthday of immortal mercy."

And the glory of his Yuletide creation is Ebenezer Scrooge, the grumpy old miser who gets a second chance when he most needs—and least deserves—one. The tale of Scrooge's transformative Christmas Eve is one of history's most winningly persuasive morality plays. In the company of stern ghosts, he sees his forsaken past, his heartless present and the cold, forgotten grave that is his future, as we watch his attitude change from disbelief to scorn to rationalization to terror.

During the author's lifetime, audiences at his wildly popular readings clamored for the story of Scrooge, and artists have been retelling it ever since. On radio, stage and screen, the irascible sinner has been interpreted countless times by actors ranging from Lionel Barrymore and Basil Rathbone to Mr. Magoo and Oscar the Grouch. When Scrooge awakens to find that he still has time enough to repent and reform, we're almost as thrilled and relieved as he is. Because we've seen more of ourselves in Scrooge than we expected—or care to admit. We, too, have fallen short of the goals of our younger selves; we've grubbed for a buck and looked away from someone in need; and if we haven't actually said, "Bah, humbug!" we probably have felt it from time to time. Scrooge's second chance assures us that we can have one, too, and not just on Christmas, but with each bright morning.

God bless us, every one!

—*By David Von Drehle*

Norman Bates

Origin: **Robert Bloch's 1959 novel *Psycho***

In the age of Adam Lanza and James Holmes, it may be difficult to fathom just how groundbreaking a psycho Norman Bates was. When he first appears in Alfred Hitchcock's iconic 1960 film, adapted from Bloch's novel, Bates seems an innocent boy-next-door as he welcomes the unfortunate Marion Crane to his isolated motel with a crooked smile and puppy-dog eagerness. But it doesn't take long for the cracks to appear. As he serves sandwiches in a parlor adorned with stuffed birds, Bates oscillates between cordial, lonely and unhinged as he talks about taxidermy ("My hobby is stuffing things"), his argumentative mother ("She needs me. It's not as if she were a maniac, a raving thing") and his philosophy of life ("We're all in our private traps, clamped in them and none of us can ever get out"). Even before the blood splatters the shower, we're knee deep in the dark side.

It was Tony Perkins' mesmerizing performance that ensured Bates would forever live under our skin. (He called it the "Hamlet of horror roles.") Strangely, the actor's life paralleled his character's: they both lost their fathers at age 5 and were abnormally close to their domineering mothers. Perkins, like Bates, carried a corrosive secret: as a closeted gay man in the 1950s, he was tortured about his sexuality and terrified that exposure would ruin him. Perhaps it was this anguish that gave him such sensitivity in the role, which he played in three sequels.

Before Hitchcock, Hollywood horror films involved fighting monsters or aliens from outer space. What is so terrifyingly novel about Bates is that his horror is internal—and the audience gets to marinate inside his disturbed head. Today's slasher films take the bullet train to crazytown, and the blood spurts with abandon. Along the way, they sacrifice the nuance, the forbidden sympathy we might feel for a tormented criminal. As Norman himself says, "We all go a little mad sometimes. Haven't you?"

Anthony Perkins in *Psycho*, 1960

Indiana Jones

Origin: The 1981 film *Indiana Jones and The Raiders of the Lost Ark*

We'll admit that Henry Walton Jones Jr., Ph.D., better known by his nickname Indiana, is not much of a hand with cattle. But you can't say he's all hat, even though his ever-present fedora is one of the distinguishing aspects of the character. There's a lot going on with Indy's headgear: it establishes him as a bit of a dandy, and it hints that he is a free spirit (American men hadn't considered hats stylish for decades before Professor Jones showed up in one). Indy's ability to hang onto his hat even while fleeing from giant boulders, fighting Nazis or escaping a zeppelin via a biplane, shows that he's unflappable. And then there are matters of high aesthetic concern—such as the fact that actor Harrison Ford is a very attractive rogue when he pulls down his brim just so.

The hat was genius, but when Hollywood pals George Lucas and Steven Spielberg cooked up the character of Indiana Jones, their real masterstroke was to make their action hero an archaeologist, a serious scholar whose knowledge of ancient arcana such as the Ark of the Covenant and the Holy Grail cloaks his exploits with a veneer of intellectual endeavor. And Indy's scholarly side gives him the Superman-ish complexity of inhabiting two characters at once, the thinker and the doer united.

Lucas and Spielberg famously drew on their shared love of old Saturday-afternoon movie serials in creating Jones, and, especially in the first film of the four-part series, *Raiders of the Lost Ark,* they got everything right: the cheesy use of a tiny plane flying across a map to convey movement, the wonderful touches of sly wit, the exotic international settings.

Talk about grave robbers: Spielberg and Lucas, the Frankensteins of Hollywood, gathered up the standard body parts of vintage serials—chase scenes, damsels in distress, offbeat villains—and brought them to thrilling new life with a jolt of 1980s film technology. Result: as TIME movie critic Richard Corliss declared, they managed to "kindle the innocent spirit of antique adventure-movie serials in a generation of kids who had never been to a Saturday matinee."

Felix O.C. Darley created this illustration of Longfellow's Hiawatha in the late 19th century

Hiawatha

Origin: Native American legends

Two Hiawathas have occupied the American imagination, in two different eras, and the distinction between them tells the tale of two very different North American civilizations. Of the first Hiawatha we know very little; he is a legendary figure whose tale was passed down by Iroquois tribes of present-day New York State. This Hiawatha was a great leader, a prophet of unity who succeeded in bringing all the peoples of the region, who were divided into Five Nations—the Mohawk, the Oneida, the Onondaga, the Cayuga, and the Seneca—into a larger union known as the Iroquois Confederacy.

This powerful political and cultural entity, also known as the Haudenosaunee, is believed to have come together centuries before Europeans came to America. Hiawatha, the legends say, was aided in his diplomacy by Deganawida, the Great Peacemaker, a holy man and prophet who took Hiawatha as his pupil.

Magical tales surround Deganawida: his mother is said to have been a virgin, and he survived three attempts to kill him in his infancy. Hiawatha, his student and ally, was more worldly and a charismatic orator. Together the two founded a union of tribes that boasted a constitution, a system of government based on the consent of the governed and a social order organized by matrilineal descent. The union made the Iroquois the dominant force in their region for centuries.

The second Hiawatha is not an expression of Native American culture. In 1855, centuries after the Iroquois Confederacy took shape, the learned Massachusetts poet Henry Wadsworth Longfellow published *The Song of Hiawatha,* an epic poem that was highly popular in its time. Its title character bears no resemblance to the legendary Hiawatha, who, if unreal, exemplified the dreams of his people. In contrast, Longfellow's creation is about as authentic as a cigar-store Indian.

The Marlboro Man, on a giant billboard in Los Angeles, 1988

SURGEON GENERAL'S WARNING: PREGNANT WOMEN WHO SMOKE RISK FETAL INJURY AND PREMATURE BIRTH.

The Marlboro Man

Origin: Advertising campaign for Philip Morris & Co., 1955

Thundering longhorns, coffee by the campfire, a rugged cowboy reining in his palomino to light up a smoke. If you're of a certain age, you'll know what comes next: the sonorous voice inviting us to, "Come to where the flavor is. Come to Marlboro Country."

The Marlboro Man was one of advertising's most evocative, successful and, in many quarters, reviled creations. Handsome, solitary, tough but with a soft spot for wayward cattle, he lived in a world in which men were men and a good smoke was always at hand.

And that's what Leo Burnett wanted you to think. The legendary adman was hired by Philip Morris to toughen up the Marlboro brand, which since 1924 had been advertised as a cigarette for ladies with the slogan "Mild as May," and which had recently been given a filter. Afraid the filter might seem effeminate, Burnett used real men in his early ads in 1955, including mechanics, hunters and cowboys. By 1957, sales increased by more than 3,000%. The spotlight soon narrowed to the cowpoke because, said brand manager Jack Landry, he "represented … a man whose environment was simplistic and relatively pressure free. He was his own man in a world he owned."

But then there's the real world. As cigarette smoke was identified as carcinogenic, tobacco ads were banned, first from TV and later from billboards. And then the Marlboro Men began to get lung cancer. Wayne McLaren, a rodeo rider featured in '70s print ads, became an antismoking advocate before he died in 1992, and after David McLean, another model, died in 1995, his heirs filed a wrongful death suit against Philip Morris. As antismoking sentiments increased, the Marlboro Man made his last ride into the sunset in 1999, cradling a smoke—and his life—in his hands.

Rosie the Riveter, by Norman Rockwell, 1943

Rosie the Riveter

Origin: A 1943 popular song of the same name by Redd Evans and John Jacob Loeb

World War II: as more and more American men went off to war, the nation needed women to do more than hoe victory gardens or volunteer at the USO. A federal publicity campaign was created that asked women— many of whom who had never worked outside the home—to put on overalls and start cranking out airplanes, machine guns and tanks. The term Rosie the Riveter was borrowed from a popular song to give a face to the movement.

In fact, Rosie was many faces, some real, some imagined. Surprisingly, the one so familiar today—the can-do woman with a polka-dot bandana and flexed biceps in the "We Can Do It!" poster—was not widely known during the war. Created by J. Howard Miller for Westinghouse in 1942, the poster was displayed for only two weeks in a Midwest factory, then forgotten for decades. The image became identified with Rosie in the early 1980s, when the poster was rediscovered and claimed as a feminist symbol.

The Rosie who truly helped the war effort was painted by Norman Rockwell and appeared on the cover of the May 29, 1943, issue of the *Saturday Evening Post.* She cut a remarkable figure—this Rosie was brawny yet lipsticked and paused for lunch with a riveting gun across her lap and her feet planted on a beat-up copy of *Mein Kampf.* Monumental and supremely self-assured—Rockwell was said to have been inspired by Michelangelo's Prophet Isaiah in the Sistine Chapel—Rosie was a new kind of woman, emanating a muscular patriotism.

Sadly, the promise Rosie represented did not outlive the war. When it ended, women were forced from the factories "for the sake of their homes as well as the labor situation," as the chairman of the National Association of Manufacturers put it, all too bluntly. *Sic transit gloria rosie.*

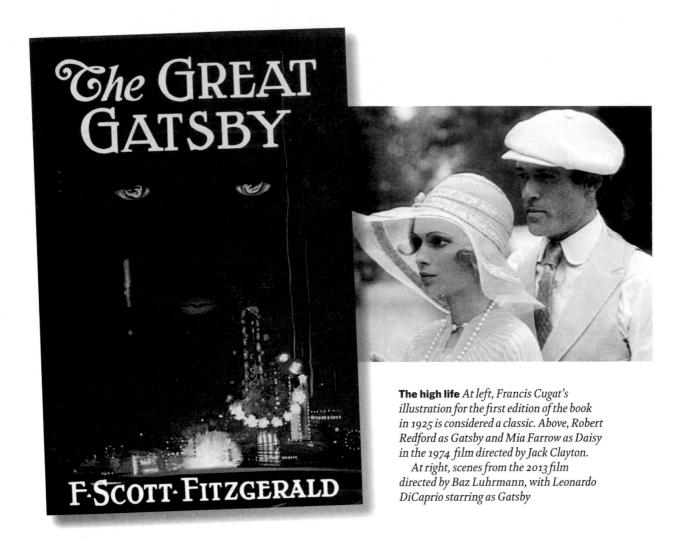

The high life *At left, Francis Cugat's illustration for the first edition of the book in 1925 is considered a classic. Above, Robert Redford as Gatsby and Mia Farrow as Daisy in the 1974 film directed by Jack Clayton.*

At right, scenes from the 2013 film directed by Baz Luhrmann, with Leonardo DiCaprio starring as Gatsby

Jay Gatsby

Origin: F. Scott Fitzgerald's 1925 novel, *The Great Gatsby*

Damn that Jay Gatsby, and damn that F. Scott Fitzgerald as well! Colluding like a couple of Wall Street insiders, they have conspired to mislead generations of Americans into buying into a bogus philosophy of life in which the pursuit of wealth and all the pleasures it can bring are elevated above all other concerns.

Of course, we are told again and again—usually beginning in high school—exactly the opposite. Our teachers stressed that Fitzgerald's classic depiction of life in the jazz age is perhaps the greatest American fable: of the futility of living for riches and pleasure, of how Gatsby's life misled should be a warning for all of us not to fall prey to the American secular religion of wanton materialism and the worship of the golden calf.

But then we meet Gatsby, at his magnificent estate on Long Island. And, like our innocent stand-in Nick Carraway, the novel's narrator, we decide that perhaps there is something to be said for the pleasures of living in a mansion on the water; of hosting glittering nights of jazz, gin and riled-up flappers; of owning lots and lots and lots of beautiful bespoke shirts. And though we know we ought to know better, we join Carraway in a mutual swoon. And we find ourselves sharing in the prayer of St. Augustine, the carefree young man of Hippo who also had a taste for high living: "Give me chastity and continence, but not yet."

Like many Americans—and like the curious antihero

of TV's *Mad Men,* Don Draper—Gatsby is a self-made man, a projection of his aspirations. Born James Gatz in a struggling household in North Dakota, he chafed in his role. In a moment of self-invention, we are told, he issued a declaration of independence—Let James Gatz *be!*—and Gatsby was born. "He invented just the sort of Jay Gatsby that a 17-year-old boy would be likely to invent, and to this conception he was faithful to the end," we learn. Gatsby is a hollow shell. Behind that magnificent façade, there's no *there* there. "I had talked with him perhaps half a dozen times in the past month and found, to my disappointment, that he had little to say," Carraway declares. The pages in the magnificent books in his magnificent library are uncut. Gatsby exemplifies the age-old American drive to equate possessions with happiness, and his life has all the depth of a bumper sticker: "He who dies with the most toys wins."

But what toys they are, and what an era it was—an age that embraced nihilism in the shadow of a world war in which an entire generation of young men were led to slaughter for reasons that no one seemed able to articulate. Is it any wonder the denizens of the jazz age embraced the allure of fast living? "The Age demanded an image/ Of its accelerated grimace," suggested the poet Ezra Pound, and in the decline and fall of the Gatsby Empire, we find ourselves along for the ride, and, like Nick Carraway, vowing to give up the headlong rush it brings. But not yet.

Tina McCulloch starred in the 2011 premiere in Toronto of *After Mrs. Rochester,* a play by Polly Teale

Mrs. Rochester

Origin: Charlotte Brontë's 1847 novel, *Jane Eyre*

What it was, whether beast or human being, one could not, at first sight, tell: it groveled, seemingly, on all fours; it snatched and growled like some strange wild animal: but it was covered with clothing, and a quantity of dark, grizzled hair, wild as a mane, hid its head and face." This is how, in *Jane Eyre,* Charlotte Brontë introduces Mrs. Edward Rochester, née Bertha Mason. Jane meets the strange wild animal on what would have been her wedding day, were it not for the pesky little detail of Rochester's intact marriage to a mentally ill sometime arsonist he keeps locked in his attic.

In *Jane Eyre,* Mrs. Rochester is less a person than a symbol. She's a kind of Expressionist double for Jane's innermost turbulent emotions and Jane's own sense of imprisonment (by gender, by lack of wealth and status), and she's a rebuke of Rochester's bad faith. After just a few brief meetings with the beautiful part-Creole daughter of a rich family in Jamaica, Rochester "had married Bertha Mason for status, for sex, for money, for everything but love and equality," as Sandra Gilbert and Susan Gubar wrote in their 1979 landmark book of feminist literary criticism, *The Madwoman in the Attic* (named in Mason's honor). She takes on more ghostlike properties in later *Jane Eyre*–inspired works, such as Daphne du Maurier's 1938 novel *Rebecca* and Jacques Tourneur's 1943 film *I Walked with a Zombie.* But Jean Rhys' 1976 *Jane Eyre* prequel novel, *Wide Sargasso Sea,* portrays a three-dimensional, flesh-and-blood character: her formative years in Jamaica, her arranged marriage, her mental breakdown and her pathway to the attic.

That pathway ends in a suicidal fall to her death in *Jane Eyre,* finally allowing Jane to write the novel's most famous line: "Reader, I married him." But that's long after the indelible scene in which Jane gazes into a mirror only to see the first Mrs. Rochester staring back at her—underscoring Brontë's persuasive idea of Bertha Mason as the raging id of Victorian womanhood. —*By Jessica Winter*

King Midas

Origin: Greek and Middle Eastern legends, circa 800 B.C.

He's the man, the man with the Midas touch." Yes, Ian Fleming's memorable James Bond nemesis, Auric Goldfinger, is the literary descendant of the original King Midas, if removed by a span of 2,800 years or so. Midas is one of the most ancient characters in this book; he is first mentioned in Greek legends that predate Homer. The lust for riches is ancient indeed, and it is memorably personified in the tale of a man enraptured by gold—which, along with diamonds, represents wealth in its sexiest form.

Historians believe there was most likely a historical antecedent for Midas: as in the legends, this Ur-Midas was a King of the land of Phrygia in Asia Minor. Many stories surround the King, but almost all of them include the motif that scholars of folktales call "the short-sighted wish." As the narrative goes, Midas is visited by the god Dionysus, the deity of intoxication and sensuality, and he affords the god such hospitality that Dionysus offers to grant any wish Midas entertains. When Midas asks for the power to turn anything he touches into gold, Dionysus warns him to think again. But Midas, overwhelmed by avarice, again expresses his wish, and the hideous consequences soon set in. First Midas touches food, which turns to metal in his hands. His rose gardens are the wonder of the world, but when he picks a bloom, he kills it. And when he inadvertently touches his beloved daughter, with the inevitable result, he realizes that his mania for gold has not only consumed him; it has also ruined the things he values most, whose wealth cannot be gauged on a scale.

The image of organic life being frozen into inert matter is a wonderful metaphor for the hard-heartedness bred by avarice; seldom has a single human impulse, greed, been characterized so powerfully. And seldom has the modern mantra "Be careful what you wish for" found such eloquent expression as in the tale of Midas.

Illustration by Walter Crane for an 1893 edition of Nathaniel Hawthorne's *A Wonder-Book for Girls and Boys*

Couples

Captain Kirk and Mr. Spock

Origin: Gene Roddenberry's 1966 TV show, *Star Trek*

Two brave men, soul brothers who seem worlds apart yet whose unity has been forged in the fire of danger and whose mission is to go where no one has gone before. That description certainly fits in the case of *Star Trek's* Captain James T. Kirk, commander of the starship U.S.S. *Enterprise,* and his First Officer, Mr. Spock, a fascinating character who straddles not only cultures but species: his father was a native of the planet Vulcan, his mother a human.

But here's where it gets interesting: a very similar description could be applied to a number of other famous fictional couples. In the early days of America, when the frontier was the driving force in shaping the future of the nation, James Fenimore Cooper's novels featured a white frontiersman who grew up among Native Americans, Natty Bumppo, who made a similar journey with his companion, the full-blooded Mohican Chingachgook. When slavery was turning America into a house divided, Mark Twain's skylarking schoolboy, Huckleberry Finn, and his unlikely ally, the runaway black slave Jim, found freedom, brotherhood and unity on a wooden raft floating down the Mississippi. And then there are Ishmael and Queequeg in Herman Melville's *Moby-Dick*—utterly unlike, they are bound by mutual devotion.

It was the literary critic Leslie Fiedler who first pointed out this recurring theme in American fiction, in the hilariously titled 1948 essay, "Come Back to the Raft Ag'in, Huck Honey!" Yes, as the title suggests, Fiedler also noted that there is often a homoerotic element between the two inseparable soulmates, who often complete each other, either psychologically or culturally. The creator of *Star Trek*, Gene Roddenberry, took the psychological route with his two adventurers, Kirk and Spock: one is a man of passion and action, the other is one of the two most famous personifications of reason without emotion in all of fiction—the other, of course, is Sherlock Holmes.

And what a pair they are! Of the two, Kirk is a bit less of an original. Handy with his fists, hot-headed but cool under pressure and a he-man with an eye for the ladies, he's a Wild Western cowboy or a big-city detective transferred to outer space. His middle name, Tiberius, gave him a bit of spice, but most of his magic arose from actor William Shatner's wonderfully droll delivery: he managed the nifty trick of both embodying his character and winking slyly it.

Mr. Spock, in contrast, is an utter original, a brilliantly conceived character whose devotion to reason and logic made for scores of compelling plots. As in Shatner's case, much of Spock's impact flowed from actor Leonard Nimoy, who convincingly portrayed a person to whom emotion was a stranger, yet whose courage and decency earned the audience's warm regard for his cold-as-ice character. Together, Shatner and Nimoy turned what could have been a formulaic sci-fi TV series into a classic of its kind, and earned a place as one of history's great fictional couples.

Captain Kirk and Mr. Spock
Elizabeth Bennet and Mr. Darcy
Benedick and Beatrice
Huckleberry Finn and Jim
Eliza Doolittle and Henry Higgins
Leopold and Molly Bloom
Romeo and Juliet
Charlie Brown and Lucy Van Pelt
Dr. Jekyll and Mr. Hyde
The Prodigal Son and His Father
Humbert Humbert and Lolita

Nimoy as Mr. Spock and Shatner as
James T. Kirk, in *Star Trek: The Motion
Picture,* 1979

Celia Johnson and Hugh Williams as Elizabeth Bennet and Mr. Darcy in a 1936 theatrical version of Austen's novel

Elizabeth Bennet and Mr. Darcy

Origin: Jane Austen's 1813 novel, *Pride and Prejudice*

They're so easy to root for, Elizabeth Bennet and Fitzwilliam Darcy. At least they are by the end of that great novel of manners, *Pride and Prejudice.* Jane Austen reveals their suitability so deliciously slowly. He's a snob, and she's a reverse snob, so—in the words of that other classic romance, *Jerry Maguire*— they complete each other.

Very little happens in *Pride and Prejudice.* People visit each other and talk and then visit each other and talk some more. Someone eventually runs away with someone else and has to be forced to marry, but that's a sideshow, heard about thirdhand. Yet for a book that is nearly all small talk, *Pride and Prejudice* is engrossing. These people, absent any need or opportunity to make a living, are really, really good at talking. Elizabeth, whom everybody likes to think is the character most like Austen, has the wit of a woman twice her age, three times her education and half her beauty. And it all comes from talking.

The book has sold 20 million copies, which is about as many people as lived in Britain in 1813, the year it was published. And it has inspired dozens of adaptations, featuring zombies and book publicists and even a wet Colin Firth.

What keeps the two-centuries-old love story so fresh is that while the external barriers that would keep Elizabeth and Darcy apart—the differences in wealth, the opprobrium of distant relatives, the supposed call of duty—have faded more or less from the modern equation, the internal barriers are alive and well.

Well-to-do introverted boy meets girl at a country party. Boy is drawn to girl but can't stand her down-home family. Girl thinks boy is an entitled jerk. Slowly, he gets over it and she gets over herself. What Elizabeth and Darcy don't see at first is that they are always the smartest two people in the room. They've learned to adapt—he by feigning indifference, she with a killer aperçu—so nobody around them notices either. Once they figure it out, it's simply a matter of time, chance meetings and some hastily matched siblings before they get together. Brainiacs everywhere can rejoice.

—*By Belinda Luscombe*

Sam Waterston and Kathleen Widdoes in a 1973 New York Shakespeare Festival production of Shakespeare's play

Benedick and Beatrice

Origin: William Shakespeare's play *Much Ado About Nothing*, circa 1598-99

The characters featured in commedia dell'arte, the popular, low-brow Italian comedies presented by traveling troupes of players, could be reduced to simple stereotypes: the wily jester, the young lovers, the elderly fool, the bragging military man. And some of William Shakespeare's characters easily fall into such categories, including Falstaff, the boastful, aging womanizer; Romeo and Juliet, the young lovers; and so on.

Beatrice and Benedick, the wonderful pair around whom the story of *Much Ado About Nothing* revolves, are examples of a popular couple in fiction and theater, the reluctant lovers. Their appeal relies on a surefire literary device: the distance between what the readers or audience members know about the events in the fiction, and what the characters themselves know. Does any reader doubt that Elizabeth Bennet and Mr. Darcy must be married? Of course not, but the delicious part is waiting for the machinery of the plot to align so that the happy pair realizes it is their fate to wed. Does anyone outside the muddled head of Professor Henry Higgins doubt that Eliza Doolittle is the enchanting answer to his proud, misguided defiance of his own emotions? Of course not!

And is there any more delightful comic play than *Much Ado About Nothing,* a sunny romp set at a time when soldiers return from the battlefield, and female hearts become a fresh object for conquest? Of course not! To add to the fun, Shakespeare makes his reluctant lovers adults of a certain age who claim to disdain love: Beatrice is a dazzlingly witty and spirited "spinster," and Benedick is a veteran warrior, a Henry Higgins in uniform, too proud to admit he is desperately in need of a wife. To watch their awkward dalliances, brilliant put-downs and elaborate verbal pirouettes is to bask in the sense that our world is a lovely piece of clockwork, timed to resolve all conflicts into a perfect outcome—a brilliant marriage and a lusty set of dances—when the curtain comes down. All the Bard's comedies celebrate marriage, sex and the promise of regeneration, but only this one dares to put the premise of comedy so prominently center stage, when Benedick, finally deciding to woo Beatrice, declares, "The world must be peopled!"

51

Huckleberry Finn and Jim

Origin: Mark Twain's 1884 novel, *Adventures of Huckleberry Finn*

They are the most unlikely of American heroes: Huck Finn, a poorly educated adolescent boy, son of the town drunk in a quiet hamlet in northeast Missouri, and Jim, a runaway African-American slave who joins him in fleeing the restrictions of society and seeking freedom. Their creator was also unlikely: after taking the pen name Mark Twain, Samuel Clemens emerged as one of the great comic observers of American life, charming readers with his easygoing fables of boyhood mischief, his tall tales of life in the West, his factual reports of his adventures on the frontier and his chronicles of hapless Yankees visiting Europe, innocents abroad. No one could have expected the popular author to write one of the towering works of American literature, or to confront head on the nation's great original sin of slavery, or to create an epic whose story is central to the nation's culture and familiar even to those who have never read the novel. But Twain did write that epic, and a river runs through it.

And what a river it was, intimately familiar to Twain from his years as a steamboat captain on the Mississippi, long before the days when the great paddle wheelers were replaced by railroads and the river's awful power and lawless ways were tamed by dams and bureaucrats. Twain's novel, set four decades before he wrote it, captures the feel of a nation and a region still raw and rugged and, like its young protagonist, still in the process of being civilized. Against that backdrop Twain places his young hero, who is an outsider to society by virtue of his youth, his impoverished background and his choice of a black slave as his companion. As the two runaways make their way down the Mississippi on a wooden raft, young Huck Finn is torn between two powerful forces: the natural trust and affection he feels for his companion, Jim, and the harsh voices of the society into which he has been born, which champion the corrupt institution of slavery.

As Huck and Jim explore the freedom of the river, Huck faces up to the decision before him: whether to help Jim escape slavery or to heed the teachings of his elders, which prescribe damnation for those who defy legal human bondage. Conscience-stricken, he composes a letter to Jim's rightful owner, admitting he has run away with her human property. But then he recalls his journey downriver with Jim, "and how good he always was." And he makes his choice: " 'All right, then, I'll go to hell'—and then tore [the letter] up." In that gesture, slavery is condemned, the deepest American values of equality are upheld, and Huck becomes a hero.

Huck and Jim, part of a mural in the Missouri State Capitol by Thomas Hart Benton

Pulling strings
*Al Hirschfeld's
1956 poster for*
My Fair Lady
*captures the
show's history*

Eliza Doolittle and Henry Higgins

Origin: Greek myths; George Bernard Shaw's 1912 play *Pygmalion*

The great musical comedy *My Fair Lady* is long removed from its sources, the Greek myth of Pygmalion and Galatea and the comedy *Pygmalion* by George Bernard Shaw. Yet it is such a winning version of the old tale that it has come to subsume its origins. For modern audiences, the charming Cockney flower girl, Eliza Doolittle, and the starchy professor of phonetics, Henry Higgins, are the embodiments of this ancient story of transformation—which itself has only profited from a series of transformations by some of history's most gifted artists.

The story has magnificent bloodlines. The original myth tells of a sculptor who creates an ivory statue of a sea nymph that is so beautiful he falls in love with it and, with the aid of Venus, brings it to life. The tale was turned into eloquent Latin verse by Ovid in his masterpiece, the *Metamorphoses.* Denounced as pagan by early Christians, that work nearly perished but survived the long centuries that followed the fall of Rome to be discovered anew in the Middle Ages, when it became very popular. The theme of the sculptor who breathes life into his work is understandably an inspiration to artists, and from the Renaissance on, countless painters have treated the story on canvas.

Enter Shaw, a wizard of wordplay who created a Pygmalion in his own image, the language-besotted master of British dialects, Higgins. The prickly professor transforms the yowling flower girl into a social sensation by training her to speak like an upper-crust British toff, even as she melts his frigid heart. Shaw's superb spoof of the British class system was in turn transformed by lyricist and librettist Alan Jay Lerner and composer Frederick Loewe into *My Fair Lady,* which Time declared a "delight" on its Broadway debut in 1956. And that—for now—ends this long, magical tale of multiple metamorphoses.

Milo O'Shea as Leopold and Barbara Jefford as Molly in the 1967 film *Ulysses,* directed by Joseph Strick

Leopold and Molly Bloom

Origin: James Joyce's 1922 novel, *Ulysses*

Mr. Leopold Bloom," James Joyce tells us as he introduces the protagonist of *Ulysses,* "ate with relish the inner organs of beasts and fowls." After bringing his wife Molly tea in bed, "Poldy" fries himself up a pork kidney. It's an earthy breakfast for an earthy man, one who is revealed to have a wandering mind. As he goes about his errands on June 16, 1904—placing a newspaper ad for work, grabbing a cheese sandwich down the pub, running into Joyce's alter ego, Stephen Dedalus—his mind roves the universe. He mulls history, ponders mortality, turns over puns, and mourns the death, years ago, of his infant son.

But always, like Ulysses' ship, his thoughts return home, to Molly, whom he suspects (rightly, it turns out) of an affair. Molly, an opera singer, has been seeing Blazes Boylan, a concert manager and fellow singer as flashy and cocksure as Leopold is staid and routine-bound. It's the oldest story in the world. What makes it

endlessly new is how Joyce's stream-of-consciousness writing slows time, capturing his characters' thoughts like time-lapse photography.

Molly gets only the final chapter to herself, and what may be the most famous last word in the English language. As Leopold slumps back to bed after his long day, she remembers their meeting, when she was an officer's daughter on Gibraltar. In eight massive, sweeping sentences, she lays out her life: her childhood, her music, her past loves and, finally, Leopold's proposal: "he could feel my breasts all perfume yes and his heart was going like mad and yes I said yes I will Yes."

It's a drunken, dizzying sentence, as full of hunger as the one that introduces us to her husband. For all their pains and troubles, heartbreaks and infidelities, the Blooms really are meant for each other: two ordinary sensualists, who know life is too rare a dish not to be eaten with relish. —*By James Poniewozik*

Romeo & Juliet

Origin: **William Shakespeare's 1590s play, based on earlier Italian poems and novellas**

Call Will what you will—a thief, a plagiarist, a magpie—but don't forget to call Shakespeare a genius, for he so thoroughly improved the tales he plundered from a host of different sources that history has absolved him of his larcenies. Only a churl would accuse this most creative user of the English language of lacking invention. After all, he had an empty theater to fill and an empty stage to people, and as Benedick declares in *Much Ado About Nothing,* "The world must be peopled."

But there's no denying that Shakespeare's theft in this play was large. The sources he drew from include many aspects of his version: the young lovers from rival families, the complicit friar, a duel to the death in the public square, the suicide pact and the vial of poison. But those tales didn't have Shakespeare's genius.

It was the first of these factors, the tale of two young people who defy their families' hatred to launch a forbidden love affair, that must have attracted the playwright's attention. From the sublimely attractive fruit in the Garden of Eden to the wicked allure of bootleg gin in the days of Prohibition, no marketing tool devised by the hand of man is quite so powerful as the tractor-beam lure of that which is forbidden.

theme of forbidden love back to the Roman poet Ovid, whose account of the illicit romance of the Babylonian lovers Pyramus and Thisbe was familiar to Shakespeare; he memorably staged a satirical version of their plight in the last act of *A Midsummer Night's Dream,* a comedy that also dates to the early days of his career. As for the names of the two houses, both alike in dignity, that drive the play's plot: both Montagues and Capulets can be found in Dante's *Divine Comedy.*

But if Shakespeare's star-crossed lovers are doomed by the illicit nature of their romance, they have, over time, come to represent an even broader form of love: the thunderbolt infatuations of the very young. Social norms have changed since the Renaissance, yet it is still bracing to hear Juliet's father, Lord Capulet, declare of her that "she hath not seen the change of 14 years." As for Romeo, when we first meet him, he is deep in the clutches of his moonstruck yearnings for another crush object, Rosaline, a fancy that is quickly put aside when he meets Juliet. Within 24 hours of that meeting, the two impetuous youngsters are wed; within three days, both are dead. Their stolen story of stolen kisses is not only a story of a forbidden love; like Othello's, it is also a tale of those who loved not wisely but too well.

Hello, young lovers *Shakespeare's play remains evergreen more than 400 years after its debut. From left: Italian painter Francesco Hayez's* The Last Kiss of Romeo and Juliet, *1823; Olivia Hussey and Leonard Whiting in director Franco Zeffirelli's 1968 film; Claire Danes and Leonardo DiCaprio in director Baz Luhrmann's 1996 movie, set in contemporary times.*

Below: Vadim Muntagirov as Romeo and Daria Klimentova as Juliet in the English National Ballet production of Sergei Prokofiev's Romeo and Juliet, *choreography by Rudolf Nureyev*

Charlie Brown and Lucy Van Pelt

Origin: Charlie: Charles Schulz's comic strip *Li'l Folks*, 1947. Lucy: Schulz's *Peanuts*, 1952

Charlie Brown running up to kick the football while Lucy prepares to snatch it away: it's the most famous image of this *Peanuts* duo together. But it's also the most misleading. Yes, he considers her the worst outfielder in the history of baseball. Yes, she once cataloged all his faults in the form of a slide show. But Charlie Brown and Lucy aren't enemies. They're opposites. And they need each other.

Charlie, Charles Schulz's bald-headed alter ego, is the more sympathetic, an angst-filled Everyman ("My anxieties have anxieties") who loses everything but hope. However many times Snoopy disrespects him, a line drive knocks his clothes off or the little-red-haired girl breaks his heart, he comes back to bring out the dog food, pitch on opening day and check the mailbox for Valentines. As Faulkner would have said of him, he endures. Albeit with a perpetual stomachache.

If Charlie Brown lacks confidence, Lucy is positively afflicted with it. She brooks no dissent, accepts no rejection (ask Schroeder) and knows no theory so half-baked she won't cite it as gospel truth. "This is an elm tree," she tells her little brother Linus on a nature walk. "Some day it will grow into a mighty oak." At first this may come across as bossy, entitled, fussbudgety. But sometimes you need the Lucys of the world to get things done. She is the life force. She's strong! She's right! She only wants what's coming to her!

Truth is, Charlie Brown needs a sounding board, and Lucy needs a project. So, to my mind, the perfect image of them is not the football kick but the two of them sitting at her psychiatric help booth. Most times, he vents and she lectures. Yet every now and then, there's a breakthrough. "You're right!" he says after one session. "You've made me see things differently. I realize now that I am part of this world. I am not alone. I have friends." She stares him down: "NAME ONE!"

She's one, of course. In a way, each of them is the other's best friend in the world. They just don't know it.

—*By James Poniewozik*

This poster, illustrator unknown, advertised an 1888 theatrical version of Stevenson's work

Dr. Jekyll and Mr. Hyde

Origin: Robert Louis Stevenson's 1886 novella,
The Strange Case of Dr. Jekyll and Mr. Hyde

The success of Robert Louis Stevenson's gothic thriller about a Scottish doctor who discovers a magic elixir that releases his suppressed, evil identity is not due to the originality of its conceit. The notion that each of us harbors secret urges that the restraints of living in society force us to repress is an old one indeed, as is the motif of transformation, a plot device as old as Cinderella and as new as Spider-Man. Haven't we all felt at some time during our childhood or adolescence that we harbor a corrupt interior doppelgänger who is just waiting to be unconfined and exposed, to our eternal shame?

Stevenson's tale did succeed: it enjoyed remarkable worldwide renown in the years after it was published, selling gazillions of copies, and it was mounted in numerous stage adaptations, where the transformation scenes made for chilling theatrical effect. Stevenson, of course, was a dab hand with a yarn, and his story rocks right along, holding us captive. But the enduring power of the story may stem from the way its central theme of hidden dualities is repeated throughout the tale.

Dr. Henry Jekyll's dual identity as Mr. Edward Hyde reflects the plight of anyone who has ever had to keep a guilty secret. And that's just about everyone. But the story also sketches an entire society that appears as polished and poised as the good doctor yet has a corrupt, darker side that lies surprisingly near the surface—just as Edinburgh and London contained great avenues that were only steps from alleys where prostitution and vice held sway. And then there is the author himself, an excitable romantic who wrote the novella while ailing and a little delirious from the effects of fever. The man who created the tale of Dr. Jekyll, it seems, just wasn't himself when he dreamed up Mr. Hyde.

Return of the Prodigal Son,
by Giovanni Francesco Barbieri
(Guercino), 17th century

The Prodigal Son and His Father

Origin: The New Testament's Gospel of Luke, 15: 11-32

Upon first hearing Jesus' parable of the Prodigal Son, I distinctly remember my Catholic grade-school reaction: the older brother got totally hosed. I mean, come on, it's one thing to forgive the younger brother, recalcitrant that he is. But did he really deserve that fattened calf when he came crawling back home to Papa, after squandering his father's wealth on hookers and Lord knows what else? Especially when Dad never even gave the dutiful senior sibling, after years of slaving away in his fields, as much as a goat for a party with his pals? Maybe as a mostly obedient—right, Mom and Dad?—older brother with a more free-spirited younger sibling, I took this injustice a bit too personally.

I'm a father now with, yes, two boys, ages 7 and 4. And they're different, just like those famous brothers in Luke's gospel. Will, my older son, is completely by the book, while Jack rebels, dabbles in naughty language and would be the safer bet to splinter off.

When rereading this Bible passage now, I honestly almost well up with tears. The story is so simple, so direct, a piece of literature that sparks your imagination. I can picture a twentysomething Jack driving his parents crazy but finding his happiness. Is there a better compliment for a fictional character than "designer of daydreams"?

Now, I understand the father's sprint—Bolt-like, for sure—to hug and kiss his lost child. Yes, put that robe over his famished body, those sandals on his filthy feet, the ring on his wilted finger. I'd turn the music up to high heavens. What child doesn't deserve forgiveness?

As for the envious older son, he'll get his calf one day. But maybe he needs to take a few more risks to earn his rewards, just like Baby Bro.   —*By Sean Gregory*

Sue Lyon as Lolita and James Mason as Humbert Humbert in the 1962 film

Humbert Humbert and Lolita

Origin: Vladimir Nabokov's 1955 novel, *Lolita*

With apologies to Oscar Madison and Felix Ungar, fiction's oddest couple by far is Humbert Humbert and Dolores Haze, the 12-year-old "nymphet" whom Humbert, an unapologetic pedophile, dubs Lolita. As a storyteller, Vladimir Nabokov can seem more interested in the shape and texture of his narrative than in the characters he moves around like pieces on a chessboard. And there is a sense, as we read *Lolita,* that Nabokov the writer—along with his creation, Humbert, our narrator—is standing just offstage, laughing at our discomfort over the sordid nature of the love story he has foisted upon us.

Lolita is many things at once: a far-fetched, deadpan tall tale; a poke in the eye of middle-class mores; an extended exercise in misguiding the reader through an unreliable narrator; a corkscrew detective story; a complex study in meta-fiction. And it's more: readers who don't know what they are getting into may find themselves discovering that, for many of its pages, it is a rapturous road novel, an enchanting tale of traveling America's blue highways across the Great Plains in search of exotic species of butterflies to capture.

Nabokov goes out of his way to assure the reader that Lolita herself is an ordinary, somewhat shallow adolescent. She comes alive only as the object of Humbert's lust, a lust that, like butterfly hunting, is directed toward possession. But of course, we must be cautious of everything Humbert tells us, for our narrator is one of fiction's greatest creations, a confidence man whose voice is so engaging that we find ourselves wincing to find we are cheering on his efforts to possess his underage dream girl. *Lolita* is a memorable novel of seduction, but it is not Lolita who is the ultimate object of Humbert's and Nabokov's pursuit: it is the reader.

Outliers

Wonder Woman

Origin: *All Star Comics* No. 8, 1941; ABC/CBS television series 1975-79

When I auditioned for the role of Wonder Woman almost 40 years ago, there were people in the industry who thought a dramatic series based on a female superhero wouldn't work with television audiences. They were additionally dubious about having a female lead carry any prime-time show. The fact that I was an unknown actress added to the network's doubts. The producers of the show fought to cast me and insisted on a pilot with a plot that was faithful to the comic-book character. Their creative vision struck a chord with the audience and endeared the show to long-time Wonder Woman fans. For me, the role proved to be life-altering, and I was proud to portray a character who crashed through intellectual and physical gender stereotypes.

I love how Wonder Woman epitomized and became a symbol of the empowerment of women. I never viewed her strength as constituting an attack on men or as an attempt to diminish them in any respect but, rather, saw her as representing women as equals. To this day, I view the character as a voice for equality as we continue the real-world fight for civil rights for all. Not surprisingly, Wonder Woman's fans, and my fans, are drawn from the entire population: female, male, straight, gay, old and young.

When an actor is fortunate to portray an iconic figure like Wonder Woman, one's persona becomes inextricably tied to the character. I try to live harmoniously with my inner Wonder Woman and hope that the character will continue to impact lives in a positive way for generations to come.

It is hard to believe so many years have passed since Wonder Woman first appeared on television. My manager recently received a touching e-mail from a young female fan who had watched the series on DVD. She told how the character changed her life and how much it meant to her. Then, as an apparent afterthought, she inquired about me: "She is still alive ... right?" Yes, I am very much alive.

While I put away my golden Lasso of Truth long ago, Wonder Woman's values and beliefs mirror my own. I support equal rights for women and the efforts of the LGBT (lesbian, gay, bisexual and transgender) community to end discrimination based on sexual orientation. I appear at LGBT events to support that struggle. I've raised my children to be free thinkers who understand that the truly free society to which we aspire requires that all citizens enjoy equal rights under the law. I think that I would have embraced these quintessential American values of equality without having played Wonder Woman, but it didn't hurt to have a very cool female superhero guiding me along the way!

—By Lynda Carter

Wonder Woman
Aladdin
Scheherazade
Superman
Batman
Dracula
Buffy the Vampire Slayer
Cinderella
HAL 9000
Darth Vader
Harry Potter
The Wicked Witch of the West
Rip Van Winkle
Pinocchio
Tarzan
Mary Poppins
Peter Pan
Phantom of the Opera
Cassandra

Carter as Wonder
Woman, 1977

Aladdin and the *jinni*,
19th century Arabic
miniature

Aladdin

Origin: Arabic folktales, translated in Antoine Galland's 1704-17 version of *The Arabian Nights*

The story of Aladdin and his magic lamp is loved around the world. The tale's irresistible hook is the enchanted lamp—or, more precisely, the genie who emerges from it, ready to do the bidding of the person who has summoned him. Genie is a transliteration of the Arabic word *jinni* (or *djinni*), and the playground sound of the English term reflects precisely what the tale of Aladdin does to the original *jinn*: it dumbs down an Islamic concept in order to serve the needs of the tale. In Islamic teaching, *jinn* are one of the three forms of creation, along with humans and angels (*jinni* is singular; *jinn* is plural). *Jinn* are spirits without form, made of fire, who have free will and can be either good or evil. But in this tale, the *jinni* is reduced to playing the part of a fixer in a turban.

Aladdin first appeared in the West in *The Arabian Nights,* the great collection of Arabic folktales gathered by Antoine Galland, the Orientalist and scholar who published them in France in the early 18th century. In preparing the tales he collected from Arabic manuscripts and by word-of-mouth, Galland often stripped the stories of their earthy eroticism and steered them in the family-friendly direction of the fairy tales created by Charles Perrault, whose charming stories were all the rage in France at the time.

The story of Aladdin is an example of one of the oldest of folktales, the story of a cunning, appealing trickster, like Odysseus, who overcomes supernatural forces through magical arts, completes a journey and wins a kingdom. In his duel with a sorcerer who seeks to fool Aladdin into doing his dirty work, Aladdin employs a magic ring that releases a genie who guides him to an even more potent magic lamp, which, when rubbed, releases an even more potent genie. After a series of deceptions, disguises and struggles for power, Aladdin defeats the sorcerer, ascends to the throne and rules over a healed kingdom—thus achieving the rewarding conclusion that is the reason we turn to fairy tales in the first place, the voyage from solitary hardship to living happily ever after in the land of Once Upon a Time.

Scheherazade

Origin: **Arabic folktales, collected in *The Arabian Nights***

Scheherazade is the narrator of the vast collection of Arabic folktales we call *The Arabian Nights,* which dazzled European readers when they first encountered it. The story of Scheherazade, which frames the other tales, can be traced to Persian sources, and it concerns a King who has been deeply wounded by the sexual betrayal of his first wife. In retaliation, he has repeatedly married a virgin every single day, forced her to tell him a bedtime story—then sent her off to be beheaded the next day. After a thousand nights of such mayhem, his latest lover/victim, the canny Scheherazade, breaks the King's spell by telling a ripping story that ends in a cliff-hanger. The King cannot behead her, or he would miss the end of the story. His fair lady completes the tale the next night, only to begin a new one, again leaving the King yearning for more yarn. After 1,000 such nights, the King realizes he loves Scheherazade—and makes her his wife.

As the narrator of one of civilization's greatest collection of stories, Scheherazade is a kind of patron saint of the art of fiction. Meta-fiction-minded authors in the late 20th century were drawn to both her use of narration to save her life and her enviably limitless inventiveness. Jorge Luis Borges and John Barth, writers fascinated by the act of storytelling, have treated her tale in their works. To meet a thoroughly modern Scheherazade, give Barth's witty 1973 novel, *Chimera,* a chance to seduce you.

Exotic: *Vaslav Nijinsky portrays the Golden Slave in Michael Fokine's ballet* Scheherazade, *set to Nikolai Rimsky-Korsakov's music, in a 1910 performance. Illustration by Georges Barbier*

Superman appeared for the first time in his own comic book in the summer of 1939

Superman

Origin: *Action Comics* No. 1, 1938

"Y ou don't tug on Superman's cape," sang Jim Croce, and that's good advice. But Superman's cape tugs at you—just as it has since the Man of Steel burst onto the American scene in 1938, the product of two young science-fiction fans, writer Jerry Siegel and illustrator Joe Shuster. Comic-book aficionados have traced the origins of the founding figure of the superhero genre back to a startling variety of influences, from Friedrich Nietzsche's Uberman to such early newspaper comic strips as *Little Nemo* and *Flash Gordon*, to the sci-fi novels of Edgar Rice Burroughs. But no one, even Shuster, could explain the origins of the Man of Steel's signature billowing cloak, the cape that launched a thousand strips. (And a lot of lawsuits, after the two sold the rights to their creation for a mere $130.)

If Superman embodies the deepest male dreams of power, he is also an avatar of transformation and wish fulfillment. Who has not felt himself to be Clark Kent, a ho-hum nebbish who can't seem to catch Lois Lane's eye, and who has not dreamed of a phone-booth makeover in which our unimpressive exterior is stripped away and our deepest dreams of our true self are made incarnate?

Superman, of course, isn't quite human: he hails from Krypton and only plays a human in the newsroom. But his status as an alien/human adds another dimension to his character: for all his unusual powers, he is doomed to remain the perennial outsider, longing to fit into the social order and be just like everyone else. This search for assimilation may have had a special resonance for Siegel and Shuster, the young Jewish men who created him and who understood the superhuman exertions it can take just to be one of the gang.

Michael Keaton in Tim Burton's film *Batman,* 1989

Batman

Origin: *Detective Comics* No. 27, 1939

B ruce Wayne, a.k.a. Batman, a.k.a. the Dark Knight, is an outlier among outliers: virtually alone among superheroes, he has no magical powers. He doesn't hail from Krypton, he wasn't bitten by a radioactive spider, and he is definitely not an Amazon princess. But he does command two essential qualities of the breed: he lives a double life, carefully concealing his adopted identity as the Batman from his "ordinary" life as Wayne, the orphaned heir to an estate worth gazillions. And he strives, unwavering in his mission, to rid this fallen world of the evil characters who would turn Gotham into a playpen of vice.

And let's not overlook one of Batman's chief attractions: like James Bond, he commands an arsenal of snazzy vehicles, wacky weapons and gravity-defying devices, all of which he stashes in his personal Fortress of Solitude, the Batcave. And then there's his character: if Superman is a square-jawed, patriotic figure who fights for truth, justice and the American way, Batman is a far darker hero, driven by his desire to achieve revenge for his murdered parents. It's the darkness in his world that also makes Batman's foes quirkier and more interesting than Superman's bad guys—and it's his suave, intellectual side that makes Bruce Wayne's Caped Crusader hip. Over the years, Batman has been portrayed on a '60s TV show as a Roy Lichtenstein canvas come to life; as the central figure of a rewarding run of imaginative Tim Burton fantasies; and, most recently, as a relentless, muscle-bound crusader in a freak-show series of action films loaded with violence. Perhaps it's time we met a kinder, gentler Batman—but don't hold your breath.

Schreck in *Nosferatu,* 1922

Dracula

Origin: Eastern European folktales; Bram Stoker's 1897 novel, *Dracula*

He first traveled beyond the confines of his native Transylvania and found much wider notoriety in the pages of Bram Stoker's novel, and Count Dracula has never looked back. He takes a place among fiction's creepiest characters, with a coffin full of scary attributes. Cursed to dwell in a state of living death, he is a vampire who keeps himself alive by drinking the blood of others, ushering some into his crepuscular world with a befanged kiss. He sleeps in a coffin, can appear as a bat or a wolf or an ethereal mist. He fears garlic and a Christian cross, and, in many tales, can only be killed with a stake through the heart. Top that, Hannibal Lecter!

At times overlooked but easily among his most delicious attributes on film is his Romanian accent. Has there ever been a voice so unctuous, so productive of goose bumps, so dripping with slime, dread and malice? And then there's his outré digs—a sublimely spooky castle perched on the loneliest tor of the Carpathian Mountains.

Small wonder, a hero's gallery of great actors have relished playing the Count, from Lon Chaney Jr. on: there have been more than 200 screen adaptations of his story, which leaves him, um, breathing down the neck of Sherlock Holmes for the most-portrayed-on-film character in this book. The spin-offs from Stoker's novel, which he based on countless ancient European legends, are many, including Count von Count from *Sesame Street* and the tale's popular recent manifestation, Stephenie Meyer's series of *Twilight* novels and the hugely successful films based on them.

But TIME joins those who argue that the greatest version of Dracula's story is among the earliest: F.W. Murnau's 1922 German Expressionist film *Nosferatu,* in which Max Schreck portrays the Count so convincingly that rumors still circulate that Schreck was himself one of the undead.

Sarah Michelle Gellar as Buffy circa 1999

Buffy the Vampire Slayer

Origin: Joss Whedon's 1992 film *Buffy the Vampire Slayer* and the 1997-2003 TV series

Talk about eternal life: in November 2010, Warner Bros. Studios announced it would create a new film based on the TV cult hit, *Buffy the Vampire Slayer,* which originated as a feature film and then ran for seven seasons on TV. But oddly enough, it was the show's partisans who were eager to drive a stake through the heart of a *Buffy* revival. Among them were TIME culture critics James Poniewozik ("I can't think of any good reason that *Buffy* needs to get rebooted") and Michelle Castillo ("I don't think it should be made").

What's the problem? In a word, provenance. The new film would not be written and directed by Buffy's famed creator, Joss Whedon. In 1997 the writer-director had turned his 1992 film about an ordinary high school girl who uses martial arts and cool weaponry to fight off a host of paranormal creepy critters into the coolest show on TV. Over the course of its run, *Buffy* became a phenomenon, winking slyly at older, hipper viewers while their younger brothers tuned in to see Buffy's hot outfits and their younger sisters tuned in to see a female superhero fight off zombies with aplomb. Here was a Wonder Woman for a new age, with similar origins; Whedon once said, "The very first mission statement of the show was the joy of female power: having it, using it, sharing it." And so it was, as Whedon pushed against the soft bigotry of low expectations endemic to network TV and created a heroine who truly reflected her time, her place and her audience.

Emile Meyer, 19th century

Edmund Dulac, 1910

Gustave Doré, 1862

Cinderella

Origin: Ancient folktales; Charles Perrault's 1697 collection, *Stories, or Tales from Past Times, with Morals*

For the modern woman, Cinderella can be hard to like. She represents an almost toxic fantasy: that one day, if an ordinary woman is beautiful enough, and finds a way to get hold of some kickass clothes and statement shoes, she will be rescued by a wealthy and powerful guy. She will be lifted out of her miserable working life and into one of luxury and prominence. Those girls who used to be mean to her will envy her and suck up to her. Happily ever after and so on.

And all because she has small feet.

This is a fairy tale, one that we share with our youngest and most impressionable females. But let's be candid: it could also be the plot outline of an episode of *Real Housewives* or *Who Wants to Marry a Millionaire?* All you have to do is take out the words *fairy* and *godmother* and replace them with *credit* and *card*.

There are some who love Cinderella, because she teaches us that we are all special, and the right guy will discover us. For the same exact reason, others hate her. Why does she have to be rescued? Could she not have parlayed her experience with fireplace maintenance into some kind of a small business? If we have to have an improbable outcome, could she not have taken the coal cinders and discovered a miraculous talent for chiaroscuro?

And yet, she has her good qualities, our Cindy. She rises above the cliché, above the limitations of her

John Hassall, 1912

Artist unknown, circa 1895

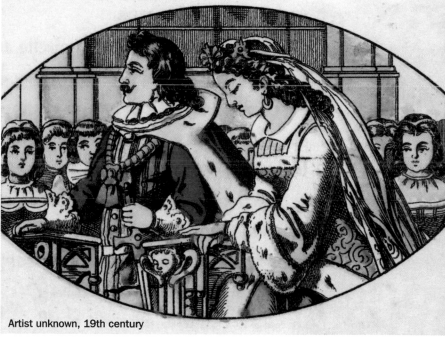

Artist unknown, 19th century

story. She's not afraid of dirty work. She's flexible; a lifetime of manual labor, and she can still talk to a prince. She's gutsy enough to not just wear glass slippers but also dance up a storm in them. And let's face it, we would all love to take the everyday things around us, if not the rat and the pumpkin, then the dishrag and the computer, and turn them into something magical. Just for one night. —By Belinda Luscombe

Ball girl *Cinderella—Cendrillon, to the French—graduated from folktale to the printed page when France's Charles Perrault told her story in his seminal collection of fairy tales at the turn of the 18th century. The Brothers Grimm published their own version in the 19th century. The tale has been illustrated by artists both little-known and famous, including Gustave Doré*

HAL the computer's interface with humans

HAL 9000

Origin: **Arthur C. Clarke's 1951 short story,** ***The Sentinel,*** **the basis for Stanley Kubrick's** **1968 film,** ***2001: A Space Odyssey***

I have seen *2001: A Space Odyssey* more than 100 times; it is the movie that sparked my interest in arts criticism, which later led me into a life of journalism. But it wasn't until I saw the masterpiece on the silver screen for the first time during its 2001 rerelease that I fully grasped the emotional absurdity at the center of this space journey: the robot's the most human thing about Stanley Kubrick's universe.

From a space station to the moon's surface to sci-fi's loneliest spaceship, *2001's* humans reveal themselves as bland, banal and monotone creations with obscure motivations and little personal history (critics claim that every Kubrick character follows this predictable, dispassionate template). And then we meet HAL 9000, a computer who expresses pride in his perfection, contempt for his human cargo and fear when the last living astronaut sets about severing his CPU. Watching that climactic disconnection scene on the big screen, with booming theatrical surround sound, is to be thrown into moral limbo. The sequence begins as a victorious moment for the human astronaut, Dave Bowman, as he reclaims possession of his ship, but then slowly slides into a terrifying execution, as a seemingly sentient being begs for his life.

Kubrick deliberately draws it out, forcing us to reckon with HAL's pleas for mercy as he cries out that he can feel his mind slipping away. Listen closely, and you will hear Dave's rhythmic breathing grow louder and erratic. I think it's a sign the executioner is having a bit of difficulty carrying out the sentence.

Apart from the extraterrestrial monoliths that dictate human evolution, HAL is the enduring mystery of *2001*. Did he kill the astronauts out of self-preservation or merely follow his programming? While the answer to that question—programming—is made clear in Arthur C. Clarke's franchise, as well as the filmed *2010* sequel, I believe there's a reason Kubrick avoided clarity. He was intrigued by the rise, and risks, of technology—how computers could function both as a tool of empowerment and weapon of destruction—and he made a film about Dave and HAL, dueling with the fate of humanity in the balance. There's a reason Kubrick looks deep into HAL's enigmatic red eye ... and then looks back at us through his fish-eye lens: HAL is the only character who gets a point of view, not just an object to behold but a character who sees. Even after 100 encounters, I'm still not sure what he's thinking. —*By Steven James Snyder*

Darth Vader stalks the ice planet Hoth in *The Empire Strikes Back,* 1980

Darth Vader

Origin: George Lucas' 1977 film, *Star Wars*

Few movie villains can justify a sequel; rarer still is the nemesis capable of captivating a crowd through a trilogy. Yet between 1977 and 1983, George Lucas conceived of one of the most ingenious archenemies ever committed to celluloid: a beast by the name of Darth Vader, who was at once supernatural samurai, Frankenstein mentor and absentee dad.

Has a fluttering cape or the simple act of breathing ever evoked such menace? Augmented by James Earl Jones' booming vocals, John Williams' thundering trumpets and those glowing red chest lights that suggested a circuit board in place of a human heart, Vader is first introduced into this faraway galaxy as some form of atmospheric disturbance. In *Star Wars'* opening chase sequence, Vader's spaceship appears to consume the rebel cruiser in its crosshairs; after a rousing shootout, our shiny black menace strolls through the fog of carnage without so much a glimpse at the fallen. Here's a villain who doesn't blink or eat, who seemingly has no capacity for fear or mercy. Vader was the original Terminator, but he used the Force, rather than Arnold Schwarzenegger's biceps, to hoist his foes into the air, choking the life out of them with his mind.

As seen through the eyes of his son Luke Skywalker, Vader is a monster. In Episode I (or, as *Star Wars* fans know it, Episode IV), Darth focuses his midi-chlorians on beheading Luke's mentor, Obi-Wan Kenobi, shattering his innocence. In the sequel, Vader reveals himself as an abusive father, demanding that Luke join the family business and slicing off his hand when he declines.

By 1983's *Return of the Jedi,* Lucas was nudging his baddie into increasingly complex psychological territory. After Vader falls on his sword to protect his boy and removes his robotic face, ensuring his death in the process, Luke is finally able to mourn the fallen mass murderer. It's a riveting arc, this rise to grace, one that's gripped successive generations of *Star Wars* fans. It was primarily the Darth Vader backstory that fueled the franchise's prequels; even in the spring of 2013, 36 years after his debut, he inspired the "Vadering" craze on Instagram, in which teens not yet alive when Vader first ruled the universe continue to act out his death grip.

—By Steven James Snyder

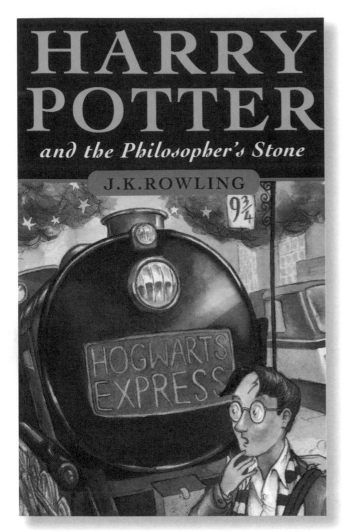

U.K. edition

Ukrainian edition

Harry Potter

Origin: J.K. Rowling's 1997 children's novel,
Harry Potter and the Philosopher's Stone

It's almost unheard of for literary characters to have as much magnitude behind their name as a Michael Jackson, a Madonna or a Barack Obama. However, Harry Potter is a rare exception.

Unfortunately, we've become so accustomed to empty promises in entertainment—pop stars who can't sing a note, actors who don't necessarily act, television personalities with surprisingly very little personality—we've trained ourselves to stop wondering why something is worthy of the attention it receives. We just

accept the current fads and suffer through until the world forgets about them.

But unlike many of the other "obsessions" he's categorized with, if you look past the hype to the actual substance, you can see that Harry Potter is worthy of the acclaim he's received. Long before J.K. Rowling's seven novels about Harry's exploits became one of the best-selling book series ever written, one of the most profitable film franchises ever produced, and a theme park that encouraged grown adults to run around in

Czech edition

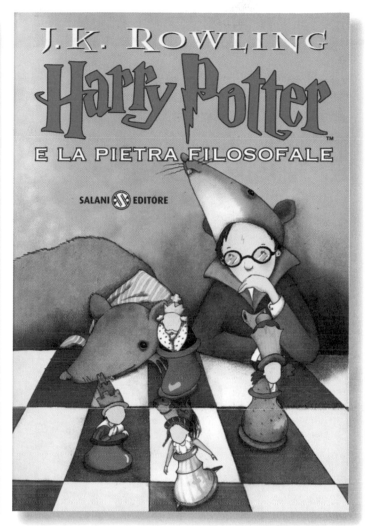

Italian edition

capes with wands (to their children's horror), Harry was just a boy who lived under the stairs, and his heroic journey into wizardry captivated the world.

In the late 1990s and early 2000s, when the *Harry Potter* books flew into bookstores, libraries and book fairs throughout the world, they brought much more than just a fantasy to readers. Harry never needed an antibullying campaign to inspire bravery. Harry and his friends never needed an outside source to validate their belief in themselves. And as the world endured

the haunting period after 9/11, it was comforting to see someone like Harry triumph over his own battle of good vs. evil.

Harry Potter taught the world to believe in magic again, that love conquers all and that the impossible can be seen as an option. It's no surprise that he is the subject of possibly the most passionate cult following of all time and that a sea of 11-year-olds is awaiting their Hogwarts acceptance letters as we speak.

—*By Chris Colfer*

Idina Menzel played Elphaba in the original
Breadway production of *Wicked*, 2003

The Wicked Witch Of the West

Origin: L. Frank Baum's 1900 children's book, *The Wonderful Wizard of Oz*

A 19th century tobacco ad featured Van Winkle

The figure of the witch is ancient indeed in human folktales. But the witches of lore and fiction are so numerous that choosing one figure to represent the sisterhood in this volume proved challenging. There's Baba Yaga, the great Slavic witch who lives in a house that stands on chicken legs. But she's not well known in the U.S. Shakespeare's witches in *Macbeth* are wonderful scene-setters for the play but are not major characters, while the fabled witches of Salem, Mass., were indeed fables, products of mass hysteria. More recently, the cold, ruthless Queen of Walt Disney's *Snow White and the Seven Dwarfs*—based on a Brothers Grimm tale—becomes a witch, but only briefly.

These days, the witch we most love to hate is the one created by L. Frank Baum in his *Oz* series of books and memorably played by Margaret Hamilton in the famed 1939 movie *The Wizard of Oz*. The Wicked Witch of the West may seem like a comic character once you've reached a certain age, but if you've watched the film with young children, you know how frightening she can be. This cackling, green-skinned harridan has lots of magical moves and commands a fleet of flying monkeys—move over, Baba Yaga.

But like most gals, even witches love a makeover, and in the past 15 years or so, the Wicked Witch of the West has undergone a major transformation. Thanks to Gregory Maguire's popular 1995 novel, *Wicked,* we've learned that the witch has a name, Elphaba (a tribute to Baum's name), that she supports a good cause (animal rights) and that she suffers from the same sort of growing pains as—surprise, surprise—all the adolescent girls who have made the musical comedy based on Maguire's book a monster Broadway hit. *Presto, change-o!* After years of drawing scorn, abuse and mockery, the Wicked Witch of the West is the witch we love the best.

Rip Van Winkle

Origin: Washington Irving's 1819 short story, *Rip Van Winkle*

Writing just as the Romantic movement was sending a thrilling current of novelty into the arts, Washington Irving seized upon several aspects of the emerging aesthetic—the new interest in national character, folktales, local color and supernatural motifs—and created two of America's most enduring fictional characters, the sleepyhead Rip Van Winkle and the gangly, gullible schoolmaster, Ichabod Crane. Irving, a fine storyteller, fondly evoked the flavor of an earlier America, the days when Manhattan was New Amsterdam, and in that region of the colonies Dutch ways still held sway.

Irving was born in 1783, in the first full flush of American Independence. He was named for the victorious general of the Revolution, and his tale of Van Winkle, if based on Dutch legend and lore, carries a surprisingly political message. It's the nature of his plight—a 20-year snooze induced by a magical brew—that captures our imagination. But Irving uses that plot device to tell a story of not only personal but also national transformation. Falling asleep while the 13 colonies are still under British rule, Rip wakes up to find his nation reinvented and the village inn sign of Britain's King repainted to show George Washington. His tale is a reminder to Americans to remember their heritage and to cherish the dawn of the nation's freedom as deeply as did those who first experienced it.

Pinocchio and Jiminy Cricket from the 1940 Walt Disney animated film

Pinocchio

Origin: Carlo Collodi's novel *The Adventures of Pinocchio*, 1883

Poor Pinocchio. The puppet protagonist of Italian author Carlo Collodi's *The Adventures of Pinocchio* and the classic 1940 Disney animated feature based on it is celebrated, above all, for one thing: the way his wooden nose grows whenever he tells a lie. Whether you're a small child or the President of the U.S., being compared to Pinocchio is never a compliment. You're being called a shameless liar. Probably an incompetent one, too—it's impossible to fool anyone when your nose gives you away every time.

The truth is that there's far more to Pinocchio's story than his tendency to dissemble, which is why Collodi's tale (originally serialized beginning in 1881 in *Giornale per i Bambini*, a children's newspaper) was a phenomenon in its time and Disney's film may be the greatest feature-length cartoon of them all. Collodi's Pinocchio is so obnoxious, in so many ways, that it's startling. (When he meets a talking, moralizing cricket—the

inspiration for Jiminy—he squashes him with a mallet.) As for Disney's puppet, he's more impressionable naif than gleeful jerk: he keeps falling in with the wrong crowd, and telling lies, because he hasn't yet learned that it's wrong to speak falsehoods.

Collodi's original serial ended in a remarkably dark manner, with Pinocchio's misdeeds leading to his being hanged by two mysterious hooded assassins. At the understandable request of his editor, the author gave the character a reprieve, writing a new conclusion in which the marionette heroically rescues his wood-carver father Geppetto, whereupon the Fairy with the Turquoise Hair—Disney's Blue Fairy—rewards him by turning him into a real boy. The film retained that happy ending. So bash Pinocchio for his dishonesty if you will, but remember this: the moral of his story is that even an incorrigible liar can turn his life around.

—*By Harry McCracken*

Tarzan

**Origin: Edgar Rice Burroughs' novel
Tarzan of the Apes, published in magazine
form in 1912 and in book form in 1914**

Like Sherlock Holmes and several other characters in this volume, Tarzan is such an irresistible character that his creator couldn't contain him. After the British orphan who was raised by apes in the African jungle made his debut in a pulp magazine, Edgar Rice Burroughs cranked out no fewer than 26 novels about him, which became increasingly desperate in their search for new plots and characters. And the loincloth-clad, vine-swinging lad went on to achieve further fame in a long procession of films and TV shows.

Burroughs was a facile writer who composed dozens of books in both the *Tarzan* and *John Carter of Mars* (a.k.a. *Barsoom)* series, and many more in genres ranging from westerns to fantasies. In the seven years it took James Joyce to write *Ulysses* (1914-21), Burroughs published some 20 novels, and the whiff of the assembly line still clings to the works of this Henry Ford of fiction.

Yet Tarzan is a great character whose allure is clear. Who has not dreamed of shedding the veneer of civilization and retiring to live in a state of prelapsarian grace in a wilder, simpler world? As Walt Whitman put it, "I think I could turn and live with animals/ They are so placid and self-contain'd."

Well, Burroughs' animals are not always placid, but the mangani apes (a species he invented) that nurture Tarzan and share his life in the jungle are deeply sympathetic. The noted primatologist Jane Goodall told the British magazine the *Big Issue* in 2012, "I read the *Tarzan* books and of course I fell completely in love with Tarzan. I felt he'd married the wrong Jane—it should have been me."

But if Tarzan managed to shed society's shackles in the jungle, his creator could not. The *Tarzan* books capture, as if in amber, the prejudices of their day, in which white Anglo-Saxon men stand atop a natural pyramid of social hierarchies, while women and those of other races cower beneath them in envy and wonder. Even then, it was a worldview nearly at the end of its rope.

Johnny Weissmuller as Tarzan in a 1939 film

Poppins, as drawn by Mary Shepard,
the character's original illustrator

Mary Poppins

**Origin: P.L. Travers' 1934 children's book,
*Mary Poppins***

It's hard to consider Mary Poppins without Walt Disney: his 1964 film adaptation of Australian writer P.L. Travers' classic children's stories was one for the ages—it won five Academy Awards and launched Julie Andrews' movie career. She and Dick Van Dyke will forever shine as the lovable nanny and the cheery chimney sweep.

The film was the product of a nonsaccharine drama played out behind the scenes, as Disney tried to secure the film rights to the character. The decades-long, transatlantic machinations could be a movie unto itself (and will be, in a film scheduled for a 2013 release, starring Tom Hanks and Emma Thompson).

The story begins in the early 1940s, when Disney's two daughters, huge Poppins fans, asked their father if he could feature Poppins in a movie. Disney approached Travers, who turned him down flat, concerned that Disney would simplify and sentimentalize her characters. Travers' Mary Poppins was indeed magical, but she could also be abrupt, strange and frightening. She was prim, not pretty.

Disney continued his courtship for some 15 years. "It was as if he were dangling a watch, hypnotically, before the eyes of a child," Travers later said. Finally, in 1959 she agreed, with demands: the movie would not be animated, and she would have final script approval.

When the film was completed, Travers was flown to Hollywood; she didn't see the movie until the premiere (against her wishes, it had an animated sequence), and she wept most of the way through. The transformation of Mary Poppins was especially vexing. "Why," she asked, "was Mary Poppins, already beloved for what she was—plain, vain and incorruptible—transmogrified into a soubrette?"

The battle for the soul of Mary Poppins goes on, as Travers' starchy nanny dukes it out with Disney's sweeter version: in the opening ceremony of the 2012 Olympics, a fleet of airborne Marys battled a 40-ft. high Lord Voldemort. The good news? Mary generally satisfies, whether you take her with or without a spoonful of sugar.

Castaway *Michael Llewelyn Davies, age 6, poses for Barrie's camera in a London park in 1906. He and his brothers, dubbed "The Castaways" by Barrie, were the inspiration for the Lost Boys in Peter Pan. Above is a poster for a 1924 movie version of the tale, which has found most success as a play or film*

Peter Pan

Origin: J.M. Barrie's 1902 novel (for adults), *The Little White Bird*

For all the giddy wonders of his fantastical life—Pirates and ticking crocodiles! Flying around with a fairy! No parents telling you what to do!—it's possible to feel a little uneasy about Peter Pan, the jerkin-clad aerial lad who is almost always played by a pixieish female onstage. There's the rampant commercialization, of course. His name has been plastered on peanut butter, an interstate bus line and, most recently, a psychological syndrome that points the finger at irresponsible child-men who refuse to grow up. More ominously, there's the association with Michael Jackson, who so identified with Peter that he named his ranch Neverland and invited "lost boys" over for slumber parties.

Through countless incarnations, Peter has often been dipped in sugar, but his creator, Scottish writer J.M. Barrie, had more complicated notions. The working title for Barrie's 1904 play that featured the character introduced two years before was *The Boy Who Hated Mothers*—reflecting, no doubt, the rejection Barrie felt as a young boy when his own mother became inconsolable after an older brother died. (In the published play, Peter "despised all mothers except Wendy.") Peter and his cadre of Lost Boys were inspired by Barrie's relationship with five engaging young brothers he befriended in London's Kensington Gardens, the children of Arthur and Sylvia Llewelyn Davies. He became their guardian after their parents' death.

Despite his shadier aspects, Peter Pan's cocky exuberance continues to charm us. For a generation of mid-century kids, that energy was exemplified by musical-comedy star Mary Martin, first in Jerome Robbins' 1954 Broadway musical and then for NBC telecasts; gymnast Cathy Rigby later had great success in the role. In a pre-special-effects era, it was an absolute thrill to see the shutters of the Darling-family nursery fling open and the magical Peter soar into view, even if the wires holding him were in plain sight.

And then there's the everlasting appeal of eternal youth. It's the rare adult, however sophisticated, who hasn't dreamt of joining Peter in Neverland:

> *And if it means I must prepare*
> *To shoulder burdens with a worried air*
> *I'll never grow up, never grow up, never grow up*
> *Not me!*

Butler and Emmy Rossum
in the 2004 film

The Phantom of the Opera

Origin: Gaston Leroux's 1910 novel of the same name

Cassandra, by the British painter Frederick Sandys, late 19th century

Scottish actor Gerard Butler played the Phantom of the Opera in Joel Schumacher's 2004 film of Andrew Lloyd Webber's musical adaptation of the classic horror novel by Gaston Leroux. He answered questions from TIME about his role:

TIME: When did you first encounter the Phantom?
Gerard Butler: Like many people of my generation, I became acutely aware of *The Phantom of the Opera* when Andrew Lloyd Webber's musical debuted in the mid-1980s, and Michael Crawford and Sarah Brightman were captivating audiences with the music of the night. You eventually learn there's a French novel, and the classic Lon Chaney movie. But it all starts with the mask.

TIME: Why does the Phantom exert such a magnetic pull on audiences?
GB: No matter who you are, where you live, what you do, that mask intrigues you. It's mysterious, elegant, romantic, frightening—all at the same time. And you're always curious: What's behind it? Some of us feel fear, some feel empathy. And it's these emotions that drive the allure of *Phantom*. The genius of Andrew Lloyd Webber was to find a vulnerability in this monster and balance his ugliness by giving him a beautiful voice. Audiences now understand the Phantom's desires, rather than being repelled by his behavior. And in the end we learn that we all wear masks of our own and must remove them in order to show our true selves.

TIME: What surprised you about playing the Phantom?
GB: I really felt sorry for him. You have to remember that he's not a monster in the traditional sense of horror movies: he's human and deeply complex. The Phantom is brilliant, talented, charismatic and has an intriguing magic about him. But he's crippled by his disfigurement. We all have something crippling us, whether it be emotional or physical. He is in so much pain—pain that comes from alienation. I tried to give him dignity, even when he's losing control.

TIME: Was there anything frightening about the role?
GB: The scariest moment for me came in my audition. I had worked with a vocal coach, and I got to a place where I was confident in my singing. But when I got to the audition and was standing across the table from Sir Andrew, my leg started shaking, because I was just so nervous. And the whole time I'm singing *The Music of the Night,* I'm wondering if Sir Andrew can see my leg shaking. When I think back about that moment, my leg still shakes a bit.

Cassandra

Origin: Greek mythology

Cassandra is the anti-Pollyanna, doomed to find that every cloud has a gray lining, every glass is half empty and every tray table is not in its upright and locked position. Like those of so many mortals in Greek legend, her life is entwined with that of the gods—to her misfortune. Daughter of Priam, King of Troy, Cassandra was renowned for her beauty and caught the attention of the god Apollo, who blessed her with the power of foresight. Yet when Apollo demanded her love, Cassandra refused—and the angry god cursed her by ensuring her prophecies would not be heeded but scorned.

In Aeschylus' tragedy *Agamemnon,* Cassandra warns the Trojans that the city will fall. No one believes her, and the city is captured. This is the part of the story we remember, but Cassandra's fate is often forgotten: after Troy's fall, she is abducted, raped and handed over to Agamemnon, leader of the united Greek force, as a concubine. But she is murdered, along with Agamemnon, by his adulterous wife Clytemnestra. And—the horror!—she had foreseen it all.

This powerful figure endures in our everyday speech, as we label anyone who warns of coming doom a "Cassandra." And her story is alive elsewhere: on the hit TV show *Homeland,* Claire Danes plays a Cassandra figure, Carrie Mathison, a CIA analyst who warns colleagues that a U.S. war hero is a traitor—to no avail. But in our modern age, when the pagan gods are dead, it would not do to say that Carrie has been afflicted by Apollo. Rather, we are told, she is bipolar. Progress?

Everyday Heroes

Lucy Ricardo

Origin: The 1951 television comedy _I Love Lucy_

There were Lucy-like characters before Lucille Ball began playing Lucy McGillicuddy Ricardo on _I Love Lucy_ in 1951. (One of them was Liz Cooper, the proto-Lucy whom Ball portrayed in the radio show _My Favorite Husband,_ which first went on the air in 1948.) There have been Lucy-like characters in the post-Lucy Ricardo era—scads of them, since _I Love Lucy_ is the situation comedy that defined situation comedies.

But there's only one Lucy: scheming, dreaming, indefatigable Lucy, the one who stomped grapes, got sloshed on Vitameatavegamin, failed to keep up with conveyor-belt chocolates and conspired—again and again and again—to elbow her way into Ricky's night-club act. It's tempting to argue that she captured early TV watchers' imagination because she was, in her own idiosyncratic way, a feminist who refused to comply with the established rules of housewifery in postwar America. There might even be some truth to it. But mostly, Lucy mattered, and matters, because she's hilarious.

That title, _I Love Lucy,_ is meaningful. Lucy can be exasperating—actually, she's exasperating on cue in every one of the show's 181 episodes, plus 13 _Lucille Ball—Desi Arnaz Shows_. Still, there's no question that Ricky adores her, that she's a good (if kooky) mother, that Fred and Ethel Mertz are her dear friends. Lucille Ball and Desi Arnaz's marriage was no storybook romance, but Lucy and Ricky had a wonderful life together. Thanks to reruns, they still do, and will forever.

In later series—_The Lucy Show, Here's Lucy_ and _Life with Lucy_—Ball played Lucy Ricardo clones who engaged in Lucy Ricardo-like antics. But there's a discomforting pathos to those Lucys, all of whom are lonely widows who torment characters played by the preternaturally irate Gale Gordon. They remind us that Lucy Ricardo is endearing—rather than pitiful and annoying—in part because she's loved.

—By Harry McCracken

Lucy Ricardo
The Little Tramp
Jo March
Homer Simpson
Rocky Balboa
Atticus Finch
Walter Mitty
Katniss Everdeen
Nancy Drew
Mary Richards
Robinson Crusoe
The Dude
Holden Caulfield
Don Draper
Pollyanna
Cliff Huxtable
Dorothy Gale
Tom Joad
Willy Loman
Oliver Twist
Josef K.

Ball as Lucy
Ricardo, 1950s

Chaplin and co-star in the 1918 film *A Dog's Life*

The Little Tramp

Origin: The 1914 film *Kid Auto Races at Venice*

Every few weeks, outside the movie theater in virtually any American town in the late 1910s, appeared the life-size cardboard figure of a small tramp—outfitted in tattered, baggy pants; a cutaway coat and vest; impossibly large, worn-out shoes; and a battered derby hat—bearing the inscription I AM HERE TODAY. An ad for a Charlie Chaplin film featuring the Little Tramp was a promise of happiness, of that precious, almost shocking moment when art delivers what life cannot, when experience and delight become synonymous, and our investments yield the fabulous, unmerited bonanza we never get past expecting.

The Little Tramp character drew upon all Chaplin's strengths: his extraordinary athleticism, expressive grace, impeccable timing and endless inventiveness. Funniest when he is most afraid, mincing and smirking as he attempts to placate those immune to pacification, constantly susceptible to reprogramming by nearby bodies or machines, skidding around a corner or sliding seamlessly from a pat to a shove while desire and doubt chase each other across his face, the Tramp is never unself-conscious, never free of calculations, never anything but a hard-pressed if often divinely lighthearted member of an endangered species, entitled to any means of defense he can devise. Faced with a frequently malign universe, he can never quite bring himself to choose between his pleasure in the improvisatory shifts of strategic retreat and his impulse to love some creature palpably weaker and more threatened than himself.

Chaplin made silent Little Tramp films after the movies learned to talk. The Tramp, it seemed, was mute not by necessity but by choice. He'd tried to protect us from his thoughts, but if the times insisted that he tell what he saw as well as what he was, he could only reveal that the innocent chaos of comedy depends upon a mania for control, that the cruelest of ironies attend the most heartfelt invocations of pathos. Speech is the language of hatred as silence is that of love.

—By Ann Douglas

Demure—for now *Illustration of Jo March by Salomon Van Abbé for a 1950s edition of* Little Women

Jo March

Origin: Louisa May Alcott's novel *Little Women*, published in two parts, 1868 and 1869

She first strode into public consciousness, exclaiming "Christopher Columbus!" and upending inanimate objects and conventions, in 1868. The Civil War had ended only a few years previously, and another battle between American citizens, for gender equality, continued to flare. Two decades earlier, a convention at Seneca Falls, N.Y., had adopted a resolution that would underpin American women's struggle for equal citizenship, inserting two key words into Thomas Jefferson's 1776 Declaration of Independence: "We hold these truths to be self-evident: that all men *and women* are created equal."

Jo March—her androgynous first name and muscular surname signal her rebel streak—is an aspiring writer and fiercely devoted sister who came concealed inside a novel with the reassuringly regressive title *Little Women,* which quickly infiltrated traditional households to give the females within a new model for their aspirations. She still captures hearts and minds. If not for Jo, I may never have aimed to be a writer or un-

derstood how to write ("I like good strong words that mean something" is a typically instructive Jo-ism).

She shaped my ideas of personal fulfilment too. "I'm happy as I am," she exclaims, after turning down her handsome, wealthy neighbor, "and love my liberty too well to be in a hurry to give it up for any mortal man." Jo set a new template for marriage, not as a frothy dream of submission but as a union of absolute equals.

A product of her time and place, Jo and her dissident spirit have resonated across 145 years and most of the planet. She's been played onscreen by at least nine actresses as diverse as Katharine Hepburn and, disastrously miscast, the porcelain Winona Ryder. She stars in Japanese anime movies. She has been commercialized and commoditized. Yet her essential message endures. Jo entered my childhood home in Middle America not only in literary form but also as a floppy rag doll, yet she taught me, above all else, to have spine.

—*By Catherine Mayer*

America's father figure takes a break

Homer Simpson

Origin: Cartoonist Matt Groening's short sketches on *The Tracey Ullman Show*, 1987

When *The Simpsons* graduated from *The Tracey Ullman Show* in 1989 and took on a life of its own as a weekly series, there was no doubt who was the star: the immensely annoying Bart was such a shocking critter that he took America by storm. Pastors, educators and parents bemoaned his antics and attitude, but Bart was a phenom—and 11 years later the editors of TIME named the twerp one of the 100 Most Influential People of the Century. But while Bart still holds down a stool at the Notoriety Bar, a subtle shift in the national mood has gradually elevated the cultural influence of Bart's put-upon dad, Homer.

Long-suffering, dumber than dirt, his chin shadowed by stubble, Homer has been part of America's family for 26 years at this writing. And somehow, along the way, we've come to love the bumbling nuclear safety inspector we used to scorn. We love him because he perseveres through whatever horrors the show's writers thrust upon him. We love him because he is utterly honest and straightforward, and because he is far more childlike and trusting than his wised-up children. Most of all, we love him because of the love he obviously feels for wife Marge and his wacky brood. Simple, reliable, sincere, the guardian and eternal symbol of the familiar word that is contained within his first name, Homer is one of fiction's most enduring and beloved Everymen.

Rocky Balboa

Origin: The 1976 film *Rocky*, starring and written by Sylvester Stallone

Rocky Balboa's head, weighed down by doubt and anxiety, falls to the pillow. The unknown fighter is taking on the champ, Apollo Creed, the next night. "The only thing I wanna do is go the distance—that's all," Rocky tells Adrian, the sheepish, bespectacled girl he met in the Philly pet store, the love of his life who is now lying next to him. He's choking up. "Nobody's ever gone 15 rounds with Creed. If I go them 15 rounds, and that bells rings, and I'm still standin', I'm gonna know then that I weren't just another bum from the neighborhood."

Rocky lost a split decision to Apollo Creed that next night at Philly's old Spectrum sports arena, but he indeed went the distance, and shouted "Yo, Adrian!" into the crowd; now, a Rocky statue stands near the Philadelphia Museum of Art steps, which he famously scaled during training. (If *Gonna Fly Now,* the Rocky theme, isn't playing in your head right now, it should be.) No matter that he isn't real. Kids gather by that statue every day, raising their arms like Rocky.

Rocky Balboa is our modern-day David, an underdog folk-hero with a heavy accent and slurred speech. After lifting the spirits of post-Watergate, post-Vietnam America, Rocky Balboa proved his worth to the world. He even toppled the Soviet Union, at the height of the Reagan-era cold war, in *Rocky IV*. Ivan Drago may have killed Creed in an exhibition bout. But Rocky wants revenge, so he chops wood, lifts boulders and sprints in the snow while training in Siberia. (Sing the montage song: "Hearts … on … fire…") Drago had no shot. Indeed, even the Russian fans cheer the American. They admire his grit.

Sylvester Stallone created the best sports movie character of all time. *Rocky* won Best Picture for 1976, and in 2011, Stallone was inducted into the International Boxing Hall of Fame, right alongside Mike Tyson. "It's not how hard you can hit," Stallone said in his induction speech. "It's how hard you can get hit and keep moving forward, because that's really what makes the difference in your life." Yo, Adrian! Rocky did it. He's part of us forever.
—*By Sean Gregory*

Sylvester Stallone as Rocky Balboa in the 1976 film *Rocky*

Gregory Peck as Finch in the 1962 film of Lee's novel

Atticus Finch

Origin: Harper Lee's 1960 novel, *To Kill a Mockingbird*

In the opening pages of Harper Lee's masterpiece, *To Kill a Mockingbird,* the captivating narrator Jean Louise ("Scout") Finch says of Atticus Finch, "Jem and I found our father satisfactory." Millions of readers have found him to be much more than that. Wise, patient, forgiving, brave, the idealized lawyer from fictional Maycomb, Ala., epitomizes that rarest of virtues: he is the man who will do what's right when the world is saying he's wrong.

As a neighbor informs the Finch children later in the book, "There are some men in this world who were born to do our unpleasant jobs for us. Your father's one of them." Atticus Finch—whose film persona, played memorably by Gregory Peck, was chosen the greatest hero in cinema history by the American Film Institute in 2003—is a man apart, a man above the rest of us. And yet, he isn't alienated from Maycomb. He loves his backward, racist, fearful community even as his heart breaks over its shortcomings.

To Kill a Mockingbird is a marvel of naturalistic fiction, vivid and credible. All except for Atticus, who is arguably too good to be true. Handsome yet chaste, speaking only pearls, a lawyer who doesn't care if he gets paid, he can face down a lynch mob without ever raising his voice. He's the best shot in the county, but too humble to let his children know it.

This might be a flaw in another hero. And it might be fair criticism to say something's wrong when the hero of our most beloved civil rights novel is a white man. But Atticus Finch endures because he was never intended to represent the real history of his time and place. He was created to challenge his country. In a time for choosing, Lee asked, Whose side do we want to be on? With each reader who has chosen to stand with Atticus Finch, America has become a little stronger. —*By David Von Drehle*

Walter Mitty

Origin: James Thurber's 1939 short story,
The Secret Life of Walter Mitty

Most of the characters featured in this book can be traced back to massive novels, frequently performed plays or major operas. It takes a special form of genius to create a character who becomes an icon within the broom-closet confines of a short story, but when the gifted American writer and cartoonist James Thurber dreamed up the character of Walter Mitty, he personified a certain sort of temperament so well in the space of 15 paragraphs that he created an instantly familiar type.

Thurber's target in his genial narrative is a middle-aged man, his best years behind him, who embraces daydreams of grandeur to escape the constant henpecking of his bossy wife. The topic may not sound that fresh, but Thurber enjoyed a unique perspective on life, and he managed to find a surprising middle ground between sympathy and scorn for his main character. The resulting tale is warm, wise and witty, starting with our would-be hero's name, a Dickens-worthy gem that captures all the fussy futility of our daydreamer's plight in four meek syllables.

Then there's the delicious presentation of the daydreams themselves, which burst upon the reader with such bright wonderment that at first we are confused as to what's happening. Weren't we just driving down a street in Connecticut? Then how did we find ourselves in a dugout in no-man's-land, while German bombers roar overhead and the *pocketa-pocketa-pocketa* of flamethrowers merges with the pounding of cannons and the *rat-tat-tat* of machine guns and it's time to make a run for it through 40 kilometers of hell …

Yeah, that's the ticket. That's how Thurber kept his readers dreaming along with Mitty, until every single heroic mirage is shattered by the intrusion of ugly, mundane, flamethrower-free normality. If you seek Mitty's direct descendant, you might try the top of the doghouse in Charlie Brown's yard, where another inveterate daydreamer holds down a position as a World War I flying ace, a Victorian novelist and a lunar astronaut. Or you might try your local multiplex, where Hollywood comic Ben Stiller will be trying to outdo Danny Kaye's 1947 take on Mitty in a film scheduled for a late-2013 release. Dream on!

The great imposter *In the 1947 film of Thurber's tale, Danny Kaye as Mitty imagined himself a cardsharp, a surgeon, a general and a gunslinger*

Lawrence as Collins' heroine in *The Hunger Games*, 2012

Katniss Everdeen

Origin: Suzanne Collins' 2008 young-adult novel, *The Hunger Games*

Teens love a rousing postapocalyptic tale (how better to channel their rage at the mess adults have made of things?), and they were positively besotted when Katniss Everdeen, the heroine of Suzanne Collins' hugely popular *Hunger Games* trilogy, took the weight of a beleaguered world onto her 16-year-old shoulders. It's not that Katniss is a superhero, though she's handy with animal traps and a bow and arrow. Nor, at first, is she a revolutionary, though she despises the plutocrats who oppress her ravaged homeland. All Katniss wants is to save her starving family—and she'll do that with whatever she's got.

When her little sister is chosen for the Hunger Games—an elaborate competition/reality show that pits children in a fight to the death as the nation watches on TV—Katniss volunteers to take her place. From there on, her life is all survival and show biz, as she gets primped for the cameras, then sent out to kill or be killed. Throughout her ordeal she is a fascinating bundle of contradictions: brutal yet pricked by self-

doubt, angry yet kind, self-involved yet displaying a fierce integrity.

This being a YA story, there's also a love triangle, but unlike another famous threesome (think *Twilight*), there's little time for flirting. Katniss spends three volumes vacillating between her handsome and devoted suitors, careful to conceal her vulnerability from the oppressors who are recording her every move.

When the inevitable movie was announced, Jennifer Lawrence, then 20 and a "rabid fan," got the plum Katniss part. The choice was controversial to some—she was thought to be too old—and Lawrence so loved Katniss that she confessed she was "terrified" of failing. But she took command of the role and helped bring in almost $700 million in worldwide box-office grosses. "This part is so special to me," she told ENTERTAINMENT WEEKLY. And then, channeling the sentiments of Katniss's army of young admirers, she added, "She's like Joan of Arc for a new generation."

Nancy Drew

Origin: The Edward Stratemeyer syndicate's 1930 young-adult novel *The Secret of the Old Clock,* by "Carolyn Keene"

Sure, she zoomed around River Heights in her blue roadster solving *The Secret of the Old Clock* and *The Clue of the Broken Locket,* but could Nancy Drew, teen sleuth, ever imagine she'd inspire movers and shakers of the free world? Among her fangirls are Supreme Court Justices (Sandra Day O'Connor, Ruth Bader Ginsburg, Sonia Sotomayor), First Ladies (Laura Bush, Hillary Rodham Clinton) and a couple of TV superstars (Barbara Walters, Oprah Winfrey)—as well as the millions of girls who have continued to inhale her mysteries since 1930.

Forty-two years before *Free to Be … You and Me,* 16-year-old Nancy outsmarted smugglers, knew her way under a car hood and rescued her chums, excitable Bess and tomboy George, from various predicaments. She made clear to Ned Nickerson, her all-American, and strangely passive, "special friend," that sleuthing would always trump romance. She was smart, coura-

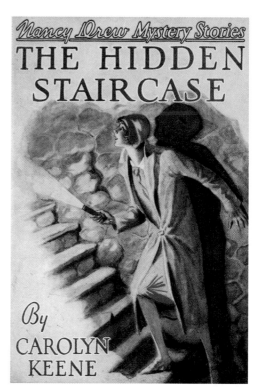

The cover of the teen sleuth's second adventure, 1930

geous and almost unimaginably independent at a time when girls' futures were terribly circumscribed. Nancy's self-reliance started early—her mother died when she was young and her attorney father was often distracted by work—but she was hardly a rebel, and her adventures always helped others.

Nancy was the brainchild of book-series publisher Edward Stratemeyer, who had enjoyed great success with the *Hardy Boys* books and wanted a series for girls. Though he died shortly after the first book launched, the franchise thrived in the hands of his daughter Harriet and ghostwriter Mildred Wirt Benson. Together they molded the yin and yang of Nancy's character. Harriet, the Wellesley grad, made sure Nancy drank tea in cloche hats and was nice to everyone, even the crooks she put in the slammer. Mildred—a trailblazing "rough-and-tumble newspaper person" and the most influential of the many writers who used the pen name Carolyn Keene—disliked the "namby-pamby" of girls' books and gave Nancy her signature pluck.

Those early books were far from perfect—they had terrible racial stereotypes that were later removed—but in many ways they represented Nancy's Golden Age. After Benson stopped writing and the '50s kicked in, Nancy lost some of her feistiness. Modern Nancy wears pants, hangs with Ned in a hot tub and, alas, drives a hybrid. But fans of vintage Nancy will never accept her in tame wheels. After reading about "her blue roadster," Justice Sotomayor once reminisced, "my having a sports car became a life dream."

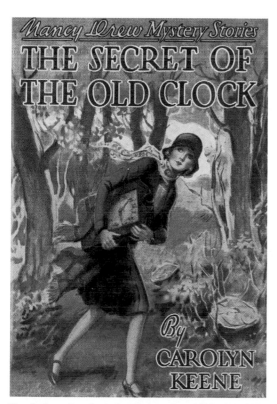

The first mystery featuring Drew was published in 1930

Mary Richards

Origin: The 1970 CBS comedy
The Mary Tyler Moore Show

At a very early age, I knew what I wanted to do with my life. But it wasn't until years later, when our production team began developing *The Mary Tyler Moore Show*, that I realized Mary Richards was the person I wanted to be. She navigated opposing personalities with charm and wit, she was fair in her relationships, she found excitement and joy in every aspect of her life, and she wasn't afraid to show vulnerability. Mary Richards had an effortless ease and likability that drew people to her, and even won over the tough but lovable Lou Grant, her boss. She had ... spunk.

As the cameras started rolling for our first season, I knew Mary Richards was special. What I didn't exactly foresee was how many women across the country would also embrace Mary. In 1970, there weren't many women like her. She was unapologetically interested in her career and found fulfillment in her life, without a husband or children. We weren't trying to change the tide, but Mary did make some waves. Behind her perfectly coifed hair, enviable wardrobe and near perfect demeanor was a woman who wanted more for herself and was going to try her best to get it. Suddenly Mary was part of a shift in our culture: she had a life many women aspired to have. She sparked conversations about glass ceilings and opened the door for women.

Through the years, I've met hundreds if not thousands of women who have told me they would dream of moving to Minneapolis, working at the WJM station and throwing their hat up in the air just as Mary did. It's lovely to see she has brought so many as much joy as she's brought me. I'm humbled to have played such an iconic character, who has had an impact not only in the world of television, but also in the lives of those who hold a special place in their hearts for Mary Richards.   —*By Mary Tyler Moore*

Moore as Richards at her TV studio workplace

Illustration from an early 20th century edition, artist unknown

Robinson Crusoe

Origin: Daniel Defoe's 1719 novel, *Robinson Crusoe*

When asked years ago what single item he would take to a desert island, my father chose cigarettes. My mother said she would take my father—provided he was allowed the cigarettes. It's easy to see their character in the answers, but there's another character hidden in the question. Every time someone uses this icebreaker, a hat should be tipped to the patron saint of castaways: Robinson Crusoe.

After Daniel Defoe shipwrecked Crusoe on a desert isle nearly 300 years ago, his story became a backdrop for every soul who is dreadfully delivered from death into isolation. Narratives of survival, whether on Gilligan's Island or some inhospitable foreign planet, are "Robinsonades." So are stories about rejecting uncomplicated middle-class moderation for uncertain adventure, as Crusoe does when he sets sail against his parents' wishes early in Defoe's book.

Crusoe is fodder for professors far beyond the English Department. James Joyce saw him as a model of British conquest, a capable expat terribly quick to subjugate his man Friday. Karl Marx saw an argument about political economy in a character who created the objects of his wealth and whose worth was defined by his labor.

The shift of values painstakingly mapped by Defoe, as Crusoe learns to see riches in goat grease rather than doubloons, is part of what makes the story perennially irresistible: there is beautiful, cruel clarity on Crusoe's island, where society's trappings disappear and even the mildest comfort is a blessing.

The significance of Crusoe goes far beyond the plot too. We take novels for granted—like nationalities or language—though there was a time when they didn't exist. Defoe's work was one of the first English novels, a controversial mix of realism and fancy that helped father modern fiction. If I could take only one thing with me to a desert island, it would most likely be a book that came in *Crusoe's* wake.

—By Katy Steinmetz

Jeff Bridges as the Dude

The Dude

Origin: Joel and Ethan Coen's 1998 film, *The Big Lebowski*

I've had a long and bizarre relationship with the Dude. When I first set eyes on the robed stoner, strutting his way through the supermarket in search of expired milk, I was a college student, giggling at this vision of laziness incarnate. At the time I tagged *The Big Lebowski* as a freak show—anchored by the ingenious trio of pothead, war vet and whiner.

But as the years ticked by, I started to eye Jeff Bridges' swagger a little differently. There's a shrewdness to the Dude that I hadn't noticed before, particularly in his ability to float through life without ever paying for a drink. Here's a guy who manages to pilfer White Russians from strangers even as he's being bullied, bruised or seduced. He cracked the code of the never-ending cocktail hour.

It was when I covered the cast's New York City reunion in 2011, celebrating the release of *Lebowski* in Blu-ray format, that I started to see something entirely new in the comedy. In the 13 years since the film's debut, I had moved to New York City and embraced the city's frantic daily routine. Now, watching the Dude fumble with his giant cell phone, panic over a severed toe and nap to the sounds of bowling pins crashing, I no longer found him lazy or pathetic but almost admirable.

For you see, life flows through the Dude like water; broke or rich, stoned or sober, bystander or ransom negotiator, he has mastered the art of rolling with the punches. The Dude is attacked by nihilists, steals a rich guy's rug, botches a ransom drop-off, impregnates a stranger, is abused by the cops and watches a best friend die—and yet through it all he shrugs, powers through and hits the bowling lanes when he needs to clear his mind.

It's hardly surprising that academics and cultural critics have rushed to write books on the bum *(The Dude De Ching)* or that the annual Lebowski Fest celebration has become as much about a state of mind as silly line readings. I started laughing at, then with, the Dude; now I wish I could be more like him. It seems every *Lebowski* fan keeps returning to the film, and its slacker hero, in the hope of learning something new. The Dude abides.

—*By Steven James Snyder*

THE CATCHER IN THE RYE

J.D. Salinger

Holden Caulfield, 2011 illustration by M.S. Corley

Holden Caulfield

Origin: J.D. Salinger's short story *I'm Crazy*, 1945

His story should be dated by now: Holden Caulfield first appeared in a *Collier's* magazine short story by J.D. Salinger in 1945 and then as the narrator of his novel *The Catcher in the Rye*, published in 1951. Times, styles and cultural norms have changed since the days when Harry Truman was President and "Joltin' Joe" DiMaggio was batting for the Yankees, but as long as there are teenagers faced with the problem of fitting into an adult world that baffles and offends them, Holden will remain their confidant and lodestar. Salinger, his creator, had a special gift for accessing the inner world of a bright, highly sensitive teen and for channeling the internal dialogue of a person "not just strongly attracted to beauty but, almost, hopelessly impaled on it," as the jacket copy for the first edition of the novel described Holden's plight.

Holden's clear antecedent in American literature is Huckleberry Finn, another young hero who narrates his own story in language that captivates us. Both young men find themselves tilting at the windmills of a hypocritical society, but Holden is even more alert

to the absurdities and contradictions of American life than was his predecessor: it is the "phoniness" of adult life that constantly appalls the 17-year-old, who finds himself adrift over the course of a long, disillusioning weekend in Manhattan.

Like the battle-fatigued narrator of Salinger's brilliant 1950 story, *For Esmé—with Love & Squalor,* Holden finds an alternative to the fallen world of adults in his idealized portrait of innocent children, personified by his younger sister, Phoebe. One of the story's most heartbreaking moments finds Holden attempting to efface the *F*-word that has been scrawled on a public wall, so that young children won't be confronted with the messy realities of sex. Of course, adult readers know there is a cure for what ails Holden: time should allow him to come to terms with all the flaws that are our inheritance as humans. But no one who has squirmed on the barbed hook of adolescence has ever declared his plight with such memorable clarity as Salinger's immortal, immature Everyteen.

Don Draper

Origin: **Matthew Weiner's television series *Mad Men*, premiere 2007**

He was born Dick Whitman in rural Illinois, though only a handful of people in his life know that fact. The son of a prostitute who died in childbirth, raised by a couple that saw him as the visible embodiment of a terrible sin, the man who would become Don Draper had a childhood that was impoverished in every meaning of the word. But like his literary forebear James Gatz—otherwise known as Gatsby—the past for Draper is a malleable material, something to be molded by his will. He begins in the Korean War, where Whitman switches dog tags with Lieut. Donald Draper after an explosion—inadvertently caused by Whitman—and assumes the dead man's identity, allowing his kinfolk to believe he'd been killed in combat. It was the ultimate fresh start—an impulse that Draper would return to whenever he felt boxed in or threatened—and he made the most of it, moving to the capital of reinvention: New York City.

First working as a used-car salesman—of course—and then hawking furs, Draper parlayed drinks with the sozzled advertising executive Roger Sterling into a job with the firm Sterling Cooper. From there, pure talent—along with the looks and charisma of a lantern-jawed Ayn Rand hero—propelled him to the top of his profession. He found the perfect wife—blond-haired, blue-eyed model Betty Hofstadt—and moved to the perfect suburban home in Ossining, N.Y. But the self-reliance and will that allowed him to utterly remake his life have a dark side: a seemingly permanent restlessness. Over the years Draper has moved from woman to woman, flirting repeatedly with running away from it all and starting over again. He helped found a new agency—Sterling Cooper Draper Pryce— out of the ashes of his old one, even as his marriage to Betty was dissolving. He found a new, younger wife, and success piled upon success. But as the years wear on the man who said his life only goes in one direction—forward—Don Draper is discovering that you can't outrun the past forever.   —*By Bryan Walsh*

Jon Hamm as Draper

Mary Pickford as Pollyanna in a 1920 film

Pollyanna

Origin: Eleanor H. Porter's 1913 novel, *Pollyanna*

One hundred years after Pollyanna Whittier burst upon the American scene in Eleanor H. Porter's novel for young people, she maintains a firm grip on the American imagination. But if you seek her, you're more likely to find her in a dictionary than in a bookstore or library, and it's been 10 years since she last headlined a TV version of her story made by ITV, a British television network. That's a step down for Pollyanna, who was first played onscreen by Mary Pickford and was portrayed by the British child star Hayley Mills in a 1960 Walt Disney movie.

Pollyanna endures as a pure archetype, a figure whose name is synonymous with a single character attribute, excessive optimism. A descendant of Voltaire's Candide, Pollyanna was originally intended to be enviably optimistic rather than cringingly shallow. When first unveiled, in an age when public discourse was awash with sentimentality, Pollyanna was a bright-eyed youngster of 11, who surmounted life's obstacles—including the temporary paralysis of her legs following an accident—through a device Porter called the "Glad Game," in which one seeks always to find life's silver linings, even amid the darkest of clouds.

Porter squeezed all the sunshine she could out of her character: she wrote a sequel and allowed other writers to create 14 more of them. There was even a Parker Brothers spin-off board game. But 1913 was the last year of peace before World War I, and by the time that brutal conflict, the Roaring Twenties, Prohibition and the harrowing 1930s had left their marks on American life, the term Pollyanna had become shorthand for one who is cloyingly, annoyingly perky.

In a cynical age whose default mode is irony, Pollyanna endures only as a negative image of her former self: the best such character in recent years was Reese Witherspoon's Tracy Flick in Alexander Payne's hilarious 1999 satire, *Election*. Flick is a scheming operator who affects a Pollyanna disposition to cloak her ambition, a little engine that knows no rest. In Pollyanna's journey from Porter's day to ours, we can chart the evolution of the American consciousness over the course of a century—from sincerity to satire.

Cosby as Huxtable, with Keshia Knight Pulliam as daughter Rudy, circa 1984

Cliff Huxtable

Origin: The NBC comedy series *The Cosby Show*, 1984-92

They both loved jazz. They both had five children, including a sweet-natured son with dyslexia and a beautiful rebel of a second daughter. They were both aging track stars with spreading waistlines, whose doting but strict wives wanted them to watch their diets. So it's tempting to think that Dr. Heathcliff Huxtable, one of TV's most iconic fathers, was simply the fictional alter ego of his creator, Bill Cosby.

In fact, Cliff Huxtable was the kind of dad Cosby never had. Cosby's real father was an unreliable drunk who joined the Navy to escape his family, leaving Cosby's mother, a long-suffering maid, to raise three boys in a Philadelphia housing project. Cosby dropped out of high school before taking correspondence courses to get into college, and he blamed the absence of a strong paternal presence for his misspent youth. So what he gave America in the funny and wise obstetrician with his colorful sweaters was what Cosby himself always wanted: a loving role model who talked to his kids about their problems rather than beating or yelling at them, and showed them how to be a good husband and a respectful child to his own parents.

For most of its eight-season run, *The Cosby Show* was watched by 20 million to 30 million households every week—numbers reached today only by election nights and Super Bowls. What subliminal impact did Cliff Huxtable and his clan have over that period? In South Africa, where the show was a hit with both whites and blacks, Nelson Mandela said it helped end apartheid. When Barack Obama was elected President, historians credited the Huxtables with preparing the country to send a black man and his family to live in the White House.

It was a poignant coincidence that *The Cosby Show* went off the air in April 1992, just as Los Angeles erupted in riots over the acquittal of the white policemen who beat a black man, Rodney King. "Can't we all get along?" King pleaded that week. For almost a decade, every Thursday at 8 o'clock, the Huxtables gave Americans of all races and creeds a sense of what unites us, not what divides us. Remember that feeling?

—*By Mark Whitaker*

Left, Judy Garland as Baum's heroine. Above, Garland with, from left, Jack Haley, Ray Bolger, Bert Lahr

Dorothy Gale

Origin: L. Frank Baum's 1900 novel, _The Wonderful Wizard of Oz_

Say this about L. Frank Baum, the wizard behind _The Wizard of Oz:_ he was a brash deceiver who looked you in the eye when he told you a lie. In the introduction to his most famous book, he declares that the dark yarns of the Brothers Grimm are not fit for young eyes, and he promises that his book "aspires to being a modernized fairy tale, in which the wonderment and joy are retained and the heartaches and nightmares are left out." Fair enough, you say, and you turn the page to find this description of Dorothy Gale's kinfolk on her Kansas farm: "When Aunt Em came there to live she was a young, pretty wife. The sun and wind had changed her, too. They had taken the sparkle from her eyes and left them a sober gray … She was thin and gaunt, and never smiled now … Uncle Henry … worked hard from morning till night and did not know what joy was."

Reader, do you have a feeling you're not in an MGM movie anymore? You're not, and that's the point: Baum's book is a far, far cry from the Technicolor dreamland that Hollywood concocted from it. And that's not a bad thing—there's a reason Victor Fleming's 1939 film remains beloved, and a rite-of-passage story that American parents share with their children.

First of all, there's Judy Garland, who brought such fresh life to the role of Dorothy that Baum's creation was left in the Kansas dust. Then there's Harold Arlen and E.Y. ("Yip") Harburg, who graced the tale with a wonderful set of songs, including that soaring ode to hope, _Over the Rainbow_ (which MGM boss Louis B. Mayer tried to cut from the film, arguing it took up too much screen time). Then there's the terrific cast: Ray Bolger and Bert Lahr, Margaret Hamilton and Frank Morgan. And there are all the other diverting characters Baum created, who somehow became even more magical on the screen than in the pages of his book.

In the end, there's only Garland as Dorothy, at 16 technically too old for the role and, as a child star in Hollywood in the 1930s, surely even older than her years. No matter: plucky, cheerful, caring and loyal, she is everything we hope we will be when the storms of life loft us into unknown realms. Baum's _Oz_ stories are not all dark, and he's an engaging storyteller whose books are still read with pleasure today. But Judy, Ray, Bert & Co. are so compelling, it's no wonder most of us pay no attention to the man behind the curtain.

Henry Fonda as Joad in the 1940 film of Steinbeck's novel

Tom Joad

Origin: John Steinbeck's 1939 novel,
The Grapes of Wrath

You could make a strong argument that it is Ma Joad, the matriarch of the family of Oklahoma farmers who are forced off their land and travel to California in search of work, who is the hero of John Steinbeck's mighty novel of the Great Depression, *The Grapes of Wrath*. But though she is the glue that holds the stricken family of Okies together, Ma undergoes no real transformation in the novel; her role is to endure. It is Tom Joad who finds his family cast out of its home and who, on his journey west, is increasingly drawn to take a stand and fight against a corrupt social order.

Tom is the prism through which the reader is ushered into Steinbeck's angry portrait of a nation that has failed its citizens in the wake of the long drought Americans remember as the Dust Bowl. As the novel begins, we arrive, with Tom, at the Joad farm to find it deserted. In the pages that follow, we travel with the Joads to California, only to find that this promised land is a sort of apartheid state in which landowners, supported by the police and the banks, keep poor workers in a form of indentured servitude. By the novel's end, Tom's social conscience has blossomed, and his revelation that we must be responsible for our fellow man is expressed in his memorable declaration: "Wherever they's a fight so hungry people can eat, I'll be there. Wherever they's a cop beatin' up a guy, I'll be there ... An' when our folks eat the stuff they raise an' live in the houses they build—why, I'll be there."

Willy Loman

Origin: Arthur Miller's 1949 play,
Death of a Salesman

Both Willy Loman's status and his destiny are indicated by his name. Arthur Miller's powerful tragedy, often called the greatest American play, takes on the challenge of creating a lofty work of art based not upon the doings of persons of high degree—kings or presidents or gifted artists—but upon those of a low man, an ordinary citizen whose life story can be summed up in shockingly few words: he grew up, he married and fathered two sons, he worked all his life as a salesman, he died.

Miller's aim is to reveal to the audience how even such a seemingly simple life resonates in sympathy with the deepest themes of the human condition: suffering, honor, despair, loss, the ties of family and the obligations of society. And Miller goes farther, making Willy a representative American who over and over again invokes the creeds by which Americans are urged to live. He must be optimistic, focused on the future, cheerful in the face of the darkest despair. As a salesman, his toughest sell is to himself, for deep down, he knows he has not found the only redemption American life sanctions: success. Nor can he accept that his two sons seem doomed to follow in his footsteps. Just as Oedipus puts his eyes out so he could no longer see the dark world he inhabits, Willy turns a blind eye to the failings of his sons Biff and Happy.

Then Miller afflicts this Job-like figure with another woe, a destiny that no one watching in the audience can avoid: the loss of dignity that accompanies old age. As Willy's mind fails, he hallucinates that his successful brother has come to visit him, he berates even his loyal and caring wife Linda, and he begins to entertain dark fantasies of taking his own life.

In Miller's deft hands, the audience is led to become just as annoyed with this aging salesman's phony dreams as are his sons—yet at the same time, we hate ourselves for harboring such unworthy thoughts. And we take to heart Linda's earnest plea: "Attention, attention must finally be paid to such a person." For we understand that if we do not pay attention to Willy's plight, who will pay attention to ours?

Lee J. Cobb as Loman in the 1949 production of Miller's play, with Arthur Kennedy, left, and Cameron Mitchell, right, as his sons

Oliver Twist

Origin: Charles Dickens' 1838 novel, *The Adventures of Oliver Twist*

The Oliver Twist I knew was not from the pages of Charles Dickens but rather from the 1968 Lionel Bart musical version, *Oliver!* (Side note: I too have considered dropping my last name in lieu of an exclamation point.) It was the first musical I was ever in, and much of that experience shaped my passion for live theater. Well, at least seven minutes of it did. Seven minutes. That's about how long I shared the stage with Oliver Twist. Because of my height, I was deemed too small to be part of Fagin's gang, a rowdy group of runaways whom Oliver encounters along his epic journey in search of love and family.

Fagin's gang appeared in numerous scenes. They had dance numbers and songs that actually furthered the plot. I, however, learned to find acceptance in my truncated stage time as a nameless, orphaned workhouse boy singing for "food, glorious food" among a group of boys dressed exactly like me.

I never would have thought to complain. During the first seven minutes of that three-hour musical, the audience didn't know which one of us scrawny, dirty boys would finally emerge from the mob to ask, "Please sir, I want some more." For those seven minutes we were all Oliver Twist. Collectively we longed for love, family, adventure and acceptance. But eventually that one lucky child actor raised his bowl and asked Mr. Bumble for "more"—and I returned to the ensemble dressing room under the stage to wait out the next 2 hr. and 53 min.

The next time I would meet Oliver was during the company bows at the end of the musical. He would be scrubbed and manicured, beaming from the applause the audience was showering upon him. He would seem so far away from me. I would watch him from across the stage, still in my sad, boring workhouse costume from the first scene.

I longed for his journey. I wanted nothing more than to "consider myself one of the family" or "learn to pick a pocket or two." I wanted to ask "Where is love?" I knew I could find it, and once I found it, I knew I could sell the hell out of that "wonderful feeling."

Oliver's well-rehearsed and choreographed story would repeat the next night and the night after that. I anticipated my small contribution to his journey, and I wondered if he knew how remarkable I found his remaining 173 min. of stage time. I envied him and turned that longing into drive. I wanted a shot at embracing the strength it took for Oliver Twist to conquer all odds and end up victorious.

You might say he was the first person who lit a fire under my ass and taught me the power of drive, of creating a destiny for myself. Or maybe it was just the kid who played him. I don't remember his name. Maybe he wasn't that good. You know what? That part should have been mine.

—*By Jesse Tyler Ferguson*

Mark Lester starred as Twist in the 1968 movie musical

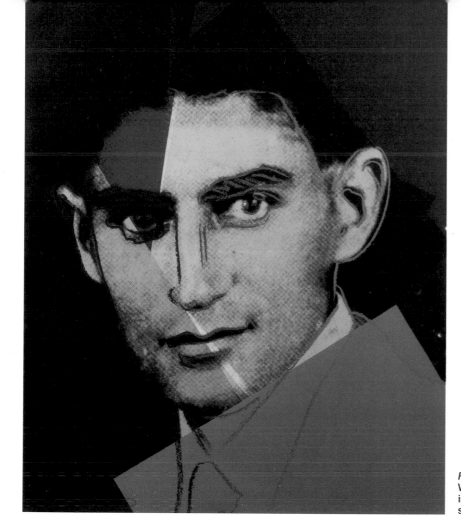

Franz Kafka by Andy Warhol, 1980; Josef K. is widely regarded as a stand-in for the writer

Josef K.

Origin: Franz Kafka's unfinished novel *The Trial*, published posthumously in 1925

"Someone must have been telling lies about Josef K., for one morning, without having done anything wrong, he was arrested." It's one of the most iconic opening sentences in all of fiction, and even though Franz Kafka began writing it in 1914, it seems to carry with it, by implication, the chilling force of all the political oppression, terror and surveillance that would follow it in the century to come.

The novel, of course, is *The Trial (Der Prozess,* in the original German), and it's the story of a man living in a drab, gray, unnamed European city who on his 30th birthday wakes up to find himself unexpectedly charged with a crime by two agents of the court. The actual charge is never specified. His accuser is never named. Josef K. attempts to deny the charges, but the legal bureaucracy by which he stands accused is so nebulous that he can't figure out how to clear his name, or defend himself, or even secure a formal trial. The charges start affecting his career as a banker. They lead him into strange, compromising sexual situations.

Gradually the legal apparatus of the court begins to invade his life, turning up in odd places—tenements, attics, his own office—becoming both inescapable yet still impossible to pin down.

As a lawyer for an insurance company, Kafka knew from bureaucracy, and Josef K.'s predicament will be powerfully familiar to anyone who has ever followed a paper trail that leads in endless, despairing circles. But Josef K. looms much larger than that: in struggling with a shadowy court system that insists on his guilt and won't even show itself to be defied, he is the avatar of millions who have lived under repressive regimes. As time goes on, his struggle seems to take on more meaning rather than less, reflecting new horrors like constant surveillance, identity theft, even drone warfare. It seems fitting somehow that Kafka never managed to finish *The Trial,* and it was only published, in fragments, after his death. Josef K.'s nightmare never truly ends either, and in the real world untold millions are still living it with him. —*By Lev Grossman*

Tragic Destinies

Hamlet

Origin: William Shakespeare's *The Tragedy of Hamlet, Prince of Denmark,* circa 1600, based on Danish legends and earlier plays

What to make of Hamlet, Prince of Denmark? He's the only son of the King, beloved of his mother the Queen and the common people of the realm, the "expectancy and rose of the fair state,/ The glass of fashion and the mould of form," in the words of Ophelia. Yet Hamlet lives in the shadow of his father, a great warrior who "smote the sledded Polacks on the ice," and seems more predisposed to quiet study than any medieval crown prince should be. At the time of his father's death, Hamlet is away from Elsinore in Germany, studying at the University of Wittenberg. It's never explained why, in his absence, the throne passed not to the crown prince, who is of age and of sound body and mind—more or less—but to the King's younger brother Claudius.

Of course, the one thing we know about Hamlet is that he always seems ready to let a good opportunity slip through his fingers. Able to think circles around everyone else in Elsinore, he nonetheless seems unable to outfox his drunken lout of an uncle. Is Hamlet hobbled by mental illness, perhaps bipolar disorder? This is, after all, someone who seems morbidly depressed to the point of suicide by the death of his father—a sad event but, as his mother notes, a common one—and then puts on an "antic disposition" that has him acting in ways that would result in strong psychoactive medication today, if not outright hospitalization. Or is he truly haunted by an apparition that, as the Ghost tells him, would "harrow up thy soul, freeze thy young blood"? Is it all in his broken mind, or does he have reason to fear that undiscovered country?

But perhaps the rottenness isn't just in Hamlet but in the royal family and in Denmark itself. Trust is nowhere to be found in Elsinore, and Hamlet is betrayed by all sides, save his university friend Horatio. Hamlet's story and life are a thwarted one, his potential cut short as much by his own limitations as his uncle's poison. Hamlet knows it as well—time and time again, in his own asides, he berates himself for his indecision and his weakness. "Thus the native hue of resolution/ Is sicklied o'er with the pale cast of thought,/ And enterprises of great pith and moment/ With this regard their currents turn awry,/ And lose the name of action." So ends Hamlet's most famous speech, with words that curdle in self-loathing. The tragedy is in him.

—By Bryan Walsh

Hamlet
Carmen
Pagliaccio
Anna Karenina
Oedipus
Madame Butterfly
Icarus
Sethe
Miss Havisham
Hester Prynne
King Lear

Laurence Olivier as
Hamlet in a 1948 film

Anna Caterina Antonacci as Carmen, 2009

Carmen

Origin: Prosper Mérimée's 1845 novella, *Carmen*

Georges Bizet drew the character of Carmen, a fiery Gypsy seductress, from a novella written by Prosper Mérimée. Mérimée's heroine would likely have been only a footnote in French literature had not Bizet touched her story with musical genius and turned her into a superstar. Mérimée was writing amid the great Romantic movement of the 19th century, and his novella, which is presented as if it were a first-person account of the author's trip to Spain rather than a piece of fiction, is a lurid postcard that wrings all the exotic local color it can from the lives of Spanish Gypsies. "She had a strange, wild beauty," the narrator/writer declares. And so Carmen does, as well as a free spirit that drives her into a knife fight with a fellow employee at a cigar factory. She then seduces a military officer, takes up with a band of smugglers and winds up besotted with a matador.

When Bizet put Mérimée's voluptuous Gypsy on the stage and showed factory workers fighting in the streets, many in the aristocratic audience revolted at the subject matter, and the opera famously failed after its premiere in 1875. But in Carmen, Bizet created a larger-than-life figure who gives singers a powerful, passionate role to play and immortal songs, like the Act I *"Habanera,"* to sing. Sultry, saucy, unapologetically living for today, Carmen is one of the first fully free women to appear on the world stage—liberated largely by virtue of her low social status—but liberated nonetheless. Society's mores, of course, demanded that she die for her loose ways before the curtain falls. Sadly, Bizet also died, at 37, only three months after *Carmen's* debut and before his work took its place as one of the most beloved of operas.

Pagliaccio

Origin: Ruggero Leoncavallo's 1892 opera *Pagliacci*

The origin of Ruggero Leoncavallo's opera is a source of some dispute. The composer claimed he based it on a true story in his family history, but French playwright Catulle Mendès claimed the Italian composer stole the story line from one of his plays. But Leoncavallo, like many other artists, appropriated his characters from the commedia dell'arte, the popular Italian comedies that feature a masked troupe of recurring characters, including the tricky, crowd-pleasing servant Harlequin; his love, the beautiful and sly Colombina; the braggart Il Capitano; and the sad clown, Pierrot, who is often presented as pining for Colombina.

Leoncavallo sets his two-act tragedy within a commedia dell'arte troupe, and the story's magic blossoms in the interplay between onstage characters and their offstage lives. As the story begins, we meet the members of the company. Canio, the head of the troupe, will play the role of Pagliaccio, a Pierrot figure. His wife, Nedda, will play Colombina. Silvio, a male romantic lead, has no role in the night's offering, a tale of adultery, but we soon learn that in real life he and Nedda are having an affair behind Canio's back.

In Act II of the opera, real life and staged life memorably collide, as the plot of the night's play mirrors the offstage drama. Canio, playing Pagliaccio, accuses Nedda, playing Colombina, of having a lover and demands to know his identity. In the climax, Canio stabs Nedda to death, then also murders Silvio, who has come to Nedda's aid. The tragedy, beautifully woven into the play-within-a-play, creates the sort of pity and horror that the Greeks called catharsis, and it makes Canio/Pagliaccio one of the most sympathetic tragic figures in all of fiction.

Enrico Caruso as Pagliaccio,
circa 1910

Greta Garbo, 1935   Vivien Leigh, 1948

Anna Karenina

Origin: Leo Tolstoy's 1877 novel, *Anna Karenina*

There's no mystery as to the source of Anna Karenina's magnetic attraction for readers: it flows directly from her creator's magnificent powers as a storyteller, a portraitist and an amused, loving, wise observer of human beings in all their strengths and failings. In 1873, four years after he published the sweeping historical novel *War and Peace,* Leo Tolstoy began writing and publishing, in serial form, a novel exploring the story of Anna, a married aristocrat highly placed in St. Petersburg society who leaves her husband to conduct an affair with a handsome young military officer, Alexei Vronsky.

Tolstoy's tale offers a compelling plot, but it is the

writer's characterizations that have made it an enduring classic. Vladimir Nabokov, who as a child met the elderly Tolstoy, identified the dueling ambitions that drove the novelist, whom he termed "a robust man with a restless soul, who all his life was torn between his sensual temperament and his supersensitive conscience." That great divide in his character ultimately led Tolstoy to renounce his art and become a prophet of Christian fundamentalism, but fortunately it also found expression in the character of Anna, who shares Tolstoy's passionate but highly self-critical nature.

In Nabokov's analysis, "Anna is a young, handsome and fundamentally good woman, and a fundamentally

Tatyana Samoylova, 1967

Keira Knightley, 2012

doomed woman." A brave, honest soul, she is too truthful to conceal her adulterous love under a cloak of secrecy, as do other society women we meet in her story. Anticipating James Joyce's *Ulysses* by some 40 years, Tolstoy makes readers the secret sharers of Anna's life by using a stream-of-consciousness narrative style that makes us feel as if we are Anna's confidants on her journey from social butterfly to scorned adulterer. Here are Anna's thoughts as she takes a carriage ride: "Long long ago, I was 17, I had gone with my aunt to the monastery there, in a carriage, there was no railway yet there. Was that really me? Those red hands? Everything that seemed to me so wonderful

and unattainable is now so worthless, and what I had then is out of my reach forever! Such humiliation. How proud and smug he [Vronsky] will be when he gets my note begging him to come. But I'll show him, I'll show him. How awful that paint smells. Why is it they're always painting buildings?"

Here, readers feel, is the very stuff of our inner lives exposed, a churning mixture of thoughts both grand and absurdly minor. But our lives are just like that, and so is Anna's—until she throws herself beneath the wheels of a train, deliberately bringing her life's story to an end. But of course, fictional characters never die, and Anna Karenina, saint and sinner, is immortal.

James Mason as Oedipus and Eleanor Stuart as Jocasta
in a 1954 production of Sophocles' tragedy *Oedipus the King*

Oedipus

Origin: Greek myths and the 429 B.C. play *Oedipus the King*, by Sophocles

The story of Oedipus is one of the most memorable of Greek myths, and it was a frequent subject for playwrights. Aeschylus' trilogy on the subject has been lost, but Sophocles' play is one of the great works of Western literature, a lofty meditation on human nature and the inflexible laws of destiny— as well as a rousing detective story that leads audiences to a thrilling catharsis, the outpouring of pity and terror that tragedy is designed to inspire.

The tale is riveting: at his birth, it is prophesied that Oedipus will kill his father and marry his mother. To avoid this destiny, his father, King Laius, abandons him on a mountainside, but Oedipus is found by a shepherd and is raised by King Polybus and Queen Merope of Corinth. Learning from the oracle at Delphi of his prophesied fate, the young Oedipus heads to Thebes, so he will not kill Polybus. On the way, he meets Laius at a crossroads; they argue, and Oedipus kills him, fulfilling the first part of his destiny. Reaching Thebes, he marries his birth mother, Queen Jocasta, fulfilling the prediction.

When a plague strikes the land, due to the incest of its rulers, Oedipus vows to find the cause of the gods' wrath. Theater holds few more thrilling moments than the scenes in which a series of messengers reveal the truth to Oedipus: in seeking to escape his destiny, he has only fulfilled it. As Sophocles has him say, "Was I not born evil?/ Am I not utterly unclean?"

He *is* unclean, for all of us are unclean, deeply flawed creatures, powerless to reverse the stern fates that shape our lives—or so the Greeks believed. And so did Sigmund Freud, who claimed that, like Oedipus, each of us is fated to want to murder one parent and marry the other.

Madame Butterfly in a 1904 publicity postcard, artist unknown

Madame Butterfly

Origin: John L. Long's 1898 short story, *Madame Butterfly*

Giacomo Puccini's opera *Madama Butterfly* failed, miserably, at its debut on Feb. 17, 1904, only to be hailed as a triumph on May 28, 1904, after the Italian composer gave it a major overhaul and staged a new version. Puccini finally stopped tinkering with the piece after five versions, and it's the final one that remains one of the most performed operas in the world.

Puccini's tale is a tragedy of cultures in collision and innocence corrupted. It is driven by the deception and treachery practiced by a young American naval officer, Lieutenant Pinkerton, against its heroine, the beautiful Cio-Cio San, who is every bit as exotic and lovely as her nation. Pinkerton, a callous villain, cynically courts, marries and impregnates the young woman, who is only 15. Then he abandons her, using a loophole in Japanese marital law to facilitate his deeds.

The wrenching tale creates enormous sympathy for the gullible Cio-Cio San as she awaits the "one fine day" on which Pinkerton will return after a three-year absence. But when he returns, it is with an American wife—and in a frenzy of grief, the "butterfly" takes her life as the curtain falls on one of the greatest closing acts in the operatic repertoire.

Icarus, by contemporary illustrator Roger Payne

Icarus

Origin: Greek mythology

"Mama always told me not to look into the sights of the sun/ Oh, but Mama, that's where the fun is." So sang Bruce Springsteen in one of his early songs, *Blinded by the Light*. Springsteen may not have been thinking about the mythological character of Icarus when he wrote those lines, but he captures the theme of the Icarus legend beautifully: the tension between pushing past barriers to enjoy life's uplift in all its soaring excitement, vs. the need to fasten your seat belt and observe the local speed limit. And if the Boss *was* thinking about Icarus, well, he was in good company: those who have referred to Icarus in song lyrics include artists as diverse as Joni Mitchell, Queen, U2, Tupac Shakur, Regina Spektor, Phish and the Indigo Girls. Led Zeppelin never featured Icarus in a song, but its members paid homage by using a representation of him as their trademark.

So … what's the link between modern rockers and the old, old tale of young Icarus and his father, the master artisan Daedalus? As the tale goes, Daedalus built beautiful wings of wax and feathers so he and Icarus could escape captivity on the island of Crete.

But when the two successfully ascended, Icarus was so struck by the joy of flight that he ignored his father's admonitions, flying so close to the sun that the wax in his wings melted, and he fell to his death in the sea.

The tale appears to have been a parable that warned Greeks against the sin of hubris, the overweening pride that brought down heroes from Oedipus to Achilles. But in modern times, many people turn the myth on its head, embracing Icarus as one whose passion for experience outpaces fusty old common sense. Icarus is often described as an inspiration to all those who risk their lives to challenge human limits, from Chuck Yeager, the man who first blew through the sound barrier, to Charles Lindbergh, Sally Ride and Neil Armstrong. For the likes of Led Zeppelin, Icarus remains appealing not as a pioneer of human endeavor but rather as an avatar of living at full tilt, without apologies. For such folk, "flying too close to the sun" is a dare to be taken, rather than a warning to be heeded. So, if Icarus is a cautionary figure of adolescent rebellion, he is also an inspiration to those who follow the counsel of William Blake: "The road of excess leads to the palace of wisdom."

Sethe

Origin: Toni Morrison's 1987 novel, *Beloved*

Of the dozen or so invented folks who tread through *Beloved,* no one, not even the novel's title character, haunts me as Sethe does. I suspect I am not alone. I have read Toni Morrison's 1987 masterpiece more than any other work of fiction. It's the narrative I've easily recommended to the broadest range of people, and the one that they all agree was the most difficult to understand, particularly Sethe's decision to slit her daughter's throat.

Even more chilling to me was the discovery that the matricide that colors the novel was based in fact. Few I've spoken to about *Beloved* knew that a real person, Margaret Garner, inspired Sethe. Like Sethe, Garner was a mother who escaped from a Kentucky plantation with her children and her mother-in-law. Like Sethe's, Garner's former owner tried to force her to return her children—who were considered stolen property—to Kentucky and into enslavement. And like Sethe, Garner killed one of her children (and was ready to murder all of her offspring) rather than have them returned to the plantation they had fled, together.

It is the brilliance and bravery of Morrison to have Beloved, quite possibly the ghost of the infant who was murdered, enter Sethe's world and expand fiction's, to me, woefully unexamined view of interior life during slavery. One of my favorite lines in the book— and there are many—is, "She love those children. She was trying to out-hurt the hurter." It speaks volumes.

I have heard from a few people that they thought Sethe's unthinkable decision was selfish, cruel and senseless. Sethe, I believe, was convinced the institution that exposed her to unimaginable inhumanity was equally, if not more so, senseless and cruel. She wasn't acting as a martyr but as a mother. Through Sethe, Morrison redefined maternal sacrifice in literature, forever. Haunting indeed.
—*By Patrik Henry Bass*

Oprah Winfrey as Sethe in the 1998 film of *Beloved*

Charlotte Rampling as Havisham in a 1999 BBC film of Dickens' novel

Miss Havisham

Origin: Charles Dickens' 1861 novel, *Great Expectations*

Charles Dickens is the master of creating characters who are such outsized avatars of basic human emotions that they have become enduring archetypes. Yet he imbues his creations with such life and detail on the page that he convinces us of their reality. Miss Havisham, the spinster who was spurned at the altar in *Great Expectations,* is one such figure. In response to her public shaming, she retreats from the world and turns her life and her home into a cobweb-clogged museum of her humiliation. In effect, she becomes her own jailer. Then, bingeing on her bitterness, she goes further, adopting a daughter, Estella, whom she turns into the agent of her revenge on men. "I stole her heart away and put ice in its place," Havisham declares.

The novel's narrator, Pip, is lured into this spiderweb of malice and becomes the victim of both women's man-hating, scornful ways. But Dickens surprises us later in the story, when he allows Havisham to realize that her lust for revenge has only added to the world's miseries, and that she has allowed the trauma of her rejection to infect the spirit of three people rather than one.

Yet if the spinster's repentance moves us, it's the haunted realm in which she dwells that fascinates us. The gloomy room, the decaying wedding cake, the hideous wedding dress, the table still set for a party that never was and never will be: these are among the most memorable images ever created of a spirit so deeply wounded that it will never heal, and for whom the past is so far from being dead, it is not even past.

Hester Prynne

Origin: Nathaniel Hawthorne's 1850 novel, *The Scarlet Letter*

America, we are often told, is a land where the future is glorious and history is bunk. Yet one of the great American writers, Nathaniel Hawthorne, was almost as besotted by the past as is Dickens' Miss Havisham. Growing up in Salem, Mass., the young man—whose forefather had been the only judge at the Salem witch trials not to repent for his actions—was struck by the ways in which the judgmental strictures of the Bay State's founding Puritan fathers continued to stunt the souls of later generations.

Hawthorne's mind was drawn to symbols and allegories, and in the scarlet letter *A* that the Puritans forced adulterous women to wear, he found a symbol that opened a window not only into Puritan culture but also into the themes of guilt and redemption that are the main concern of *The Scarlet Letter*. And in Hester Prynne, the flawed yet heroic main character of the book, he created a figure who wins the reader's sympathy for her refusal to judge herself by the values of the society around her. We first meet her when she is led to the stocks to endure hours of public shaming, yet she subverts the meaning of the scarlet *A* by embroidering it with threads of gold—and she wins our hearts.

We sympathize with Prynne because we know that, like her, we have been guilty of succumbing to passion rather than reason. We marvel at her resolve as she faces the scorn of her small-minded neighbors. We admire her refusal to play her assigned role in the Puritans' relentless machinery of guilt, shame and punishment—and we applaud her decision to raise her daughter Pearl outside the harsh bigotries of a cold religion. In the long journey of American women to escape old restraints, the scarlet letter is a red badge of courage.

Prynne in a mid-19th century engraving, artist unknown

King Lear in the Storm,
drawing by George Romney,
late 18th century

King Lear

Origin: William Shakespeare's play *King Lear,* circa 1605, based on legends of early Britain

The exact King Lear of Shakespeare's towering tragedy never lived, but some version of him did in ancient times, back when England's monarchs had guttural Anglo-Saxon handles like Brutus and Bladud and Rud Hud Hudibras. In his *History of the Kings of Britain,* the historian-*cum*-legend-maker Geoffrey of Monmouth attributed a 60-year reign to Lear (or Leir); Shakespeare used that work as a blueprint for his own drama, which also borrowed from Edmund Spenser's *The Faerie Queene* and Philip Sidney's long poem *Arcadia.* The result all but explodes with terror (of aging, of abandonment, of one's own parents and children) and pity (of the aged, of the abandoned, of one's own parents and children). *King Lear* achieves an excruciating transcendence for its title character, who begins the play using up the last of his power, and spends the rest of it howling at the consequences of his own foolishness.

To wit: blinded by his own hubris, Lear decides to divide his kingdom among his three daughters, but not before they shower him with praise. Goneril and Regan, the Bad Sisters, oblige him with overweening, disingenuous tributes; Cordelia, the Good Sister, refuses to play along. Her father—vain, short-tempered and perhaps losing his mind—disowns Cordelia in a rage, setting in motion a series of shocking episodes that produce a *Hamlet*-height stack of corpses by play's end. These events are also a terribly magnificent canvas for an actor of a certain age, who must move from resplendent smugness to fiery anger, from pleading desolation to despondent mania to, finally, a quietly deranged death scene in which the culprit is a broken heart.

The role of Lear is huge, unfathomable; Shakespeare scholar Harold Bloom went so far as to call it "unactable." Good thing that so many gifted actors have proved him wrong: in recent years, Lear has provided late-career triumphs for the likes of Ian Holm, Ian McKellen and Derek Jacobi, each of whom made audiences feel acutely "how sharper than a serpent's tooth it is to have a thankless child." —*By Jessica Winter*

Contributors

F. Murray Abraham has appeared in more than 80 films, including *Amadeus,* for which he received the Academy Award for Best Actor, and more than 90 plays. In 2013, he was honored with the Moscow Art Theatre Award.

Patrik Henry Bass is editorial projects director at *Essence.* He is the author of *Like a Mighty Stream: The March on Washington, August 28, 1963* (2002).

Gerard Butler made his stage debut as a child actor in *Oliver!* He starred as the Phantom of the Opera in the 2004 film and as King Leonidas in *300.* His many other films include *Lara Croft: Tomb Raider.*

Chris Colfer is a Golden Globe–winning and two-time Emmy– and SAG Award–nominated actor for his role on *Glee.* His first novel, *The Land of Stories,* debuted at No. 1 on the New York *Times* best-seller list in the children's chapter books category. He was named to the 2011 TIME 100 list.

Ann Douglas has taught cultural studies at Columbia University since 1975. She is the author of *The Feminization of American Culture* (1977) and *Terrible Honesty* (1995), which tells the story of jazz age Manhattan. Her current project, *Noir Nation,* focuses on U.S. culture 1940-60.

Michael Duffy is an executive editor at TIME, reporting on politics from Washington.

Jesse Tyler Ferguson is a three-time Emmy nominee for his work on ABC's *Modern Family.* He is the co-founder of the nonprofit organization Tie the Knot, which raises funds on behalf of the LGBT community through the sale of bow ties.

Jodie Foster won the Academy Award for Best Actress for her role as Clarice Starling in *The Silence of the Lambs,* and she has acted in and directed a host of other films. She was given the DeMille Award at the Golden Globes ceremony in 2013.

Sean Gregory is a senior writer at TIME, covering sports. He has written profiles of such major sports figures as LeBron James, Peyton Manning and Roger Goodell.

Lev Grossman is the book critic at TIME. He is the author two New York *Times* best-selling novels, *The Magicians* (2009) and *The Magician King* (2011).

Belinda Luscombe is an award-winning journalist at TIME. As the chief interviewer for TIME's 10 Questions page, she talks to famous people every week. She has found them to be less fun than people who don't exist, but more talkative.

Catherine Mayer is TIME's Europe editor and the author of the 2011 book *Amortality: The Pleasures and Perils of Living Agelessly.*

Harry McCracken is an editor at large for TIME. Technology is his primary beat, but in the past he has edited an animation fanzine, reviewed horror movies and contributed to *The 100 Greatest Looney Tunes Cartoons.*

Mary Tyler Moore won six Emmy Awards for her starring roles in *The Dick Van Dyke Show* and *The Mary Tyler Moore Show,* and she was nominated for the Academy Award for Best Actress for her work in the film *Ordinary People.*

Ann Patchett is the author of six novels and three books of nonfiction. She lives in Nashville, Tenn., where she is the co owner of Parnassus Books. Her new book, *This Is the Story of a Happy Marriage,* will be published in November 2013.

James Poniewozik is the TV and media critic for TIME and writes the magazine's *Tuned In* blog.

Steven James Snyder is an assistant managing editor at TIME, where he oversees digital editorial content and contributes to TIME's arts coverage.

Katy Steinmetz is a writer-reporter in TIME magazine's Washington bureau, where she covers politics and culture.

Patrick Stewart is an award-winning Royal Shakespeare Company actor. He and Ian McKellen will perform Harold Pinter's *No Man's Land* and Samuel Beckett's *Waiting for Godot* on Broadway in the fall of 2014.

David Von Drehle is an editor at large for TIME and author of *Rise to Greatness: Abraham Lincoln and America's Most Perilous Year* (2012).

Mark Whitaker is the former editor of *Newsweek,* Washington bureau chief for NBC News and managing editor of CNN. His upcoming biography of Bill Cosby is scheduled to be published in 2014.

Jessica Winter, former culture editor at TIME, is a senior editor at *Slate.* Her writing has appeared in the New York *Times,* the Boston *Globe,* the *Guardian* and many other publications.